THE BAFFLED PARENT'S GUIDE TO
FIX-IT DRILLS for
SOCCER

Robert Koger

New York   Chicago   San Francisco   Lisbon   London   Madrid   Mexico City
Milan   New Delhi   San Juan   Seoul   Singapore   Sydney   Toronto

Library of Congress Cataloging-in-Publication Data

Koger, Robert L.
    The baffled parent's guide to fix-it drills for youth soccer / Robert L. Koger.
       p.   cm.
    ISBN 978-0-07-162866-2 (alk. paper)
    1. Soccer for children—Training.   I. Title.

 GV944.2.K65   2009
 796.334'083—dc22   2008054053

1 2 3 4 5 6 7 8 9 10 11 12 13 14 15 16 17 18 19 20 21 22 23 24 25 DOC/DOC 0 9

ISBN 978-0-07-162866-2
MHID   0-07-162866-5

McGraw-Hill books are available at special quantity discounts to use as premiums and sales promotions or for use in corporate training programs. To contact a representative, please visit the Contact Us pages at www.mhprofessional.com.

This book is printed on acid-free paper.

Contents

Preface

Soccer is often thought of as a contest with people either playing offense or playing defense. Anyone who goes into coaching the game of soccer with that philosophy is doomed to fail. All players must be skilled at both offense and defense, and have the ability to switch back and forth as the ball changes possession.

If you have a new team or a team that is not performing properly, it can become a very long and frustrating season. Quite often you are only able to run a few practices before playing your first game. You don't have adequate time to teach your players much of anything. As a result you feel the pressure to get your team into shape as fast as you can. The problem with this is that you are limited by what the players have learned prior to coming to your team. Unfortunately, the players might not know much and it will require you to start from scratch. Not all players are created equal, and you will have some that are better than others. You might also have players who are natural athletes, but these players are few and far between. You will normally have players who don't have the basic skills but want to play, are willing to learn, and can be taught the skills, techniques, and tactics of the game of soccer.

There are steps that can be taken to train your players and shore up your offense or defense. There is no real quick fix if your players lack basic skills, but there are quick fixes if they have the skills but are just not executing them properly.

The first thing you have to do is to determine what aspects of your team's game are weak and what aspects it does well. Some of the information can come from watching the team play in an actual game. However, you will have to run an assessment of your players' abilities to determine who will be best in each position and what you need to do to improve each one's soccer ability.

As you go about training your team, you must remember that the actual procedures behind offense and defense are more complex than just two separate types of play. Every player on the field must be able to control his or her area using skills that are peculiar to his or her situation and position. The field is split into three basic areas, the defense, midfield, and the offense. These are terms that are more suitable to a location on the field than actual play. In reality all players on the field must be able to play offense and defense. You cannot have players that are offense or defense only.

To properly train your players, they must understand and be able to execute the skills and techniques associated with positions and situations on the field. Within every location on the field there are some techniques that are the same and there are some techniques that require a different knowledge from other player positions to properly execute a good offensive or defensive play.

Within each technique a subset of skills is required. No game strategy can be effective if you are unable to execute all levels of skills and techniques. This book is designed to help you improve your players' skills and to properly execute the correct tactics and techniques. This is done step-by-step. Chapter 1 starts with information every coach needs—information on the basic laws of the game and an explanation of the layout of the playing field. Chapters 2 through 5 explain the roles of parents and players, the equipment needed, how to assess your players for their level of skill and needs, and how to continue to train using warm-up and cooldown drills and techniques.

Chapters 6 and 7 are the heart of the book. Meant to be used as diagnostic and resolution tools, these chapters list the most common problems your team is likely to experience. These problems are then followed by explanations on how to correct the deficiencies and the suggested drills to work on with your team to solve the problem.

Chapters 8 through 13 illustrate the drills used to correct problem deficiencies. Each chapter covers a different skill, tactic, or technique. Chapter 14 covers conditioning drills to get your team in shape and keep them there. Chapter 15 is all about position play and formations. Because the whole purpose of training is to improve the skills of the players, while they and you have fun, Chapter 15 also includes some fun drills and games to use with your team. The book ends with a complete glossary to explain soccer terms and technology.

Use this book as a maintenance manual. Identify the problem, find the corrective action, and then make the repairs. Using the information here will save you work and eliminate the headaches that come with a team that doesn't properly perform.

Acknowledgments

No book can be produced without the help of many people. Writing is an individual act, but then come the parts where many other people get involved. The Chamein Canton Literary Agency has stayed with me and represented me superbly. I would like to thank Chamein for all her hard work on my behalf. I would also like to thank the outstanding people from McGraw-Hill. It takes many people to bring a book together, but three people who I had constant contact with are Ron Martirano, Nancy Hall, and the copyeditor who went word by word to make the book perfect, Sharon Honaker.

During the writing of this book, I went back to the soccer field. I signed up as a trainer for a local team and used every drill to ensure each was accurate and produced the proper results. This would not have been possible without the help of the Red River Soccer Association, which allowed me to provide training sessions for the league coaches and serve as a trainer for their teams.

A special thank you goes to Sanger United soccer team's Coach Sherri Lyons and Assistant Coach David Lyons, who graciously allowed me to step in as a trainer for their team. The coaches, the players, and the parents were all great. The players worked hard and showed a marked improvement over the season. As a result I would like to thank the players: Dakota Branch, Triston Branch, Adolfo Chacon, Beth Encizo, Logan Freeman, Tyler Gallardo, Aren Hettler, Kyle Johnson, Joseph Mayhue, Lane Melott, Xavier Nubine, Carlos Renteria, Ryan Skenesky, and Brett Youngblood. To all of the original and new Sanger, Texas, players, thank you for your hard work and great attitude.

No acknowledgment is complete without recognizing my wife, Mary. She is my in-house editor, staunchest supporter, and most ardent critic. Without her patience and understanding I would not be able to do what I enjoy so much, writing books that can help improve coaches and players in the game of soccer.

CHAPTER 1

General Information

Aspects of soccer that do not directly relate to teaching the skills, tactics, or techniques are important in the development of your team. You must know the laws of the game, the layout of the field, player positions, and even the simple terms associated with the game. As you practice with your team, teach this information to your players so they, too, can become familiar with all aspects of the game.

Laws

Every soccer league will have amendments to the laws of the game. Many coaches refer to the laws as rules, and that's fine as long as you understand they are in fact laws that define the play of the game.

Most leagues also have websites where you can find schedules, points of contact, and other information. The website will often carry the league's amendments to the laws, and these amendments are usually listed by age group. You must familiarize yourself with these laws and amendments to ensure you are training your players for the correct level of play. If you don't have access to the Web, contact your league's director of coaches.

It is also helpful if you can learn the full laws of the game. Youth soccer leagues amend and change the laws to make them apply to children playing the game. Each soccer organization has its local bylaws. Becoming informed of these laws is a must for every coach. The more you know about the laws, the better you will be able to coach. There are different ways you can do this. You can volunteer to attend a referee training class sponsored by your league, or you can purchase a rule book and read up on the laws. Another way is to go online to the Fédération Internationale de Futbol Association's website, fifa.com, and type in "laws" in the search box. This will bring you to the laws, which you can review as written, or for specific guidance, go to the site's question-and-answer section.

Field Layout

You and your players need to know the layout of the field, as shown in Figure 1.1, and be able to call the different areas by their correct names. The players will be able to learn as you progress through your practices if you repeatedly refer to each area by its correct name and occasionally add the meaning of that name.

Center Circle

The game starts or restarts inside the center circle. The team kicking can be inside the center circle to kick off. However, the opposing team must stay outside the circle until the ball is put into motion by the team that has the ball.

The offensive team places the soccer ball on the center mark, or spot, and puts the ball in motion to start play. The ball must be touched by a second player, from either team, before the player that originally started the ball in play can touch it again.

Center Mark

Inside the center circle there is a mark, which may be a circle, an X, or a short line. This mark indicates the exact center of the center circle, and it is where the ball is placed for kickoffs to start or restart play.

Figure 1.1   Field Layout

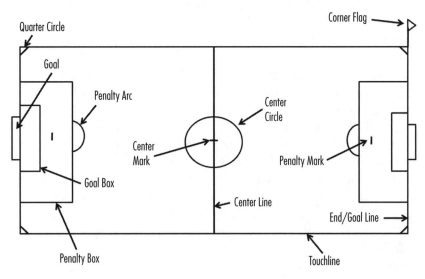

Center Line

The center line divides the field into two equal halves widthwise. At the start or restart of play from the center circle, each team is required to stay on its half of the center line until the ball is put into play.

Touchline

The touchline is the line that marks the side of the field. Field players can restart play by throwing the ball in while standing outside the touchline.

Some younger teams are required to place the ball on the ground outside the touchline and kick the ball into the field to restart play. All older players are required to throw the ball into the field to restart play.

The team that did not kick the ball out of bounds over the touchline will restart play by throwing in the ball.

End Line/Goal Line

The end line is at each end of the field and runs from corner to corner. The end line goes through the goal. However the portion of the end line that is within the posts of the goal is specifically referred to as the goal line. Whenever the ball goes outside the limits of the field, the ball is out of play and the game must be restarted.

A restart after the ball has gone out of play over the end line is done by placing the ball in the goal box and kicking it out of the penalty box if the ball was kicked out of play by the offense. This is a goal kick. If the ball was kicked out over the end line by the defense, play is restarted by placing the ball into the quarter circle at the corner of the field by the offense and kicked into the field of play. This is a corner kick.

Quarter Circle

There is a quarter circle marking in each of the four corners of the field. Play is restarted when the player kicks the ball out of the quarter circle into the field of play.

Goal Box

The goal box is the small box closest to the goal. When the ball has traveled over the end line after last being touched by the offense, or the team trying to score in that goal, play is restarted by the team defending the goal. This is done by placing the ball inside the goal box and kicking it outside the penalty box.

Penalty Box/Penalty Arc

The penalty box is the marked box at each end of the field that incorporates the goal box. The goalkeeper may use his or her hands anywhere inside the penalty area. Part of the penalty box is also the penalty arc. This arc is located on the outside center of the penalty box and is marked to ensure that all players are at least 10 yards away from the ball during a penalty kick, described below.

Penalty Spot or Mark

The penalty mark is inside the penalty box and is centered directly in front of the goal. A penalty kick is taken when there is a direct penalty against the team defending that particular goal. When a penalty kick restarts play, the referee places the ball on the designated mark and a player from the team fouled takes the kick. Any player on the field at the time of the penalty can take the kick.

The referee will signal when the kick can be taken. The goalkeeper cannot move from the goal line until the ball has been kicked and play restarted. All players except the goalkeeper and the player kicking must stay outside the penalty box, including the penalty arc, until the ball has been kicked.

Corner Flag

The corner flag is actually a small triangular flag mounted on a flexible pole placed inside each of the corner quarter circles where the touchline and end line connect. The purpose of this corner flag and pole is simple. It enables the field players to be able to see the extreme limits of the field, even when they can't see the touchline or end line.

Goal

A soccer field has two goals, one placed at each end of the soccer field. The goal is physically located in the center of the ends of the field, with the front goalposts placed directly on the end line. The net and goal frames are off the field. The goal frame is made of two side posts and a crossbar as well as frames to connect the net, which covers the back of the goal and stops the ball when kicked into the goal.

The goal line, which runs from goalpost to goalpost, is used to determine when a goal is scored. To be considered a goal and count as a score, the ball must travel completely over the goal line.

CHAPTER 2

Getting Started

Before you can train your players, you need to get yourself organized. Organization cannot be overemphasized; it is the key to running a successful program. You have to organize your equipment, lay out a practice outline, and pick a set of drills that will bring your team to the level of play you desire. You also have to let the players and parents know what you have planned for the season. Be straightforward and frank with them. Doing this will save you many headaches throughout the season.

Parents

Addressing the parents is a must. This needs to be done early in the season and is best if done prior to the first practice. You will have some type of idea what to expect by just looking at the makeup of your players and their level of experience. If you have a new team and players that have not played before, then you can count on having to train the basics. As a result you probably will not be posting check marks in the win column as fast as if you had an experienced, trained team.

   If your team has moved up into a new age group and they are the youngest team, you will also have to train them into the new level of play. It can be something as simple as moving up an age group and now having the offside rule apply. It will take a while for you to be able to get this concept across to the players. Before you do, they are going to get caught offside numerous times.

   The parents need a true assessment from you on how you think the season will go. Don't be overoptimistic if you don't really feel it. If it is going to be difficult to bring the players up to speed, let the parents know. The important thing to remember is that you are training the players, and with each training session they will improve. You will be able to see the differences on the field and so will the parents.

Parents want their children to play on winning teams, and many parents want their child to be the star, even if that child lacks the skills. However, if you tell the parents that your team is not up to par with most of the other teams, they will hear you and most of them will understand. If you tell the parents that you are going to place the players in positions best suited for them, they may not be pleased but will accept it when they see their child playing well.

Players

The first time you address the players, let them know what you expect from them and what they can expect from you. It is imperative that you establish your authority. You are not their best friend, you are their coach. Coaches don't play, they observe, train, and demonstrate, none of which requires the coach to become a player. If a demonstration is required, do it quickly and then let the players do it with you observing and correcting as necessary.

During practices you are going to have players who want to be there and players who are there because their parents want them to be there. It is up to you to make all of the players want to be soccer players. This isn't hard to do if you make the practices fun and the players learn.

The players will be looking to you for guidance. Don't tell them to do something and then you do the opposite. Always be on time, be ready to go by the time they get to the field, and stay with the schedule of drills, tactics, or techniques you decided to work on during that practice.

If you do not know how to do a specific technique yourself, don't try it. Explain it to the players, and then let them try it. It's very possible you might have someone on the team who knows how to do the specific technique.

You will have good practices if you are properly prepared. However, sometimes things just won't go as designed. Press on with practice, because it's not the end of the world. If you stay enthusiastic, so will your players.

When you address your players for the first time, be sure to introduce yourself to everyone even if most of your players are returning. Let the players know that your practices are going to be a set format and they won't just be standing around. You also need to let them know that making mistakes is okay. Even professional players make mistakes. Your players will learn through mistakes made on the practice field as well as during a game. Tell them when they make a mistake, they should press on. People learn from mistakes, and only players who stand around and do nothing don't make mistakes.

Tell them the things you expect. The players will look to you for guidance, and if you are consistent, they will follow your lead. You can pick your own issues that you think are the most important, but the major items for most coaches are being on time, never disagreeing with the referees, and never getting mad.

Be on Time

The players must be on time for practices and the games. You have preestablished a schedule for the practices and a lineup for the games. If players arrive late, it can impact the whole process.

Never Disagree with the Referee

Let the players know that the referee is always correct. It doesn't matter what the call is. If a call is questionable, you, as the coach, will handle it. However, be aware that you are not going to change the referee's call. During a game you will have calls that go against you and some that favor you. That is part of the game. Getting upset with the referee takes you and your players away from what they should be doing.

Never Get Mad

Some players will get bumped, tripped, or pushed or will have other things happen. If they get mad, then they are effectively off their game and of no value to the team. If this happens, pull them out of the game and let them sit on the bench until they are able to cool off and regain their composure.

Sometimes players from the same team will start getting on each other, especially if they are losing. This is never acceptable, and players need to know that there are consequences for their actions. Again, pull them out and sit them on the bench. Players have to understand that getting mad is never acceptable.

Equipment

Each player must have his or her own ball, shin guards, and adequate shoes and clothing. You cannot let a player practice or play in a game without shin guards. You will need a few extra balls because there will be times when some of the players will show up without one.

Cones are a must. It is recommended that you have at least 12 tower cones and 12 saucer cones. You will need both for your drills. A whistle is also a necessity. It will save your voice and also get the players used to listening to the whistle during game play. Whistles come in different styles. The most common in soccer either hang around your neck or your wrist.

You will also need a waterproof bag for your equipment. If you don't have a waterproof bag, carry a large plastic trash bag inside your equipment bag. You can then put your equipment bag into the plastic bag when necessary. You will need a clipboard and a field layout board you can draw on to show your players what you want. The clipboard and field layout board should be separate. Most are on separate sides of the clipboard. If you have a clipboard with a field layout pictured on the same side, you will always be moving your papers to get to the field layout.

Having a board with the field layout on it enables your players to get a better perspective of what you are asking. Do not draw in the dirt, because the players won't understand and you will be wasting your time and theirs. Getting a board that uses chalk will ensure that you don't run out of marker just when you need it most. If you can't find a chalk-type board, make sure you have extra dry erase pens.

Having practice jerseys is also an advantage. These may be colored vests or shirts. Either way you will need enough to have half the team in one color and the other half in another color. This allows you to distinguish two teams of players during some drills, as well as offense and defense practice.

Equipment Needed

Soccer balls, two minimum

Cones, tower and saucer, 12 of each minimum

Whistle, wrist or neck type

Soccer bag, waterproof or use a trash bag as a cover

Clipboard, any style that is easy for keeping your papers

Field layout board

Practice shirts/vests, two different colors to form two teams

CHAPTER 3

Assessing Your Players

Not all players are created equal. Some players will have talent and can be trained very easily, and other players will lack the ability to progress rapidly. How do you figure out who is who? The easy way is through some simple drills that will demonstrate enthusiasm, speed, anticipation, attitude, awareness, and skill. You will also be able to use these drills to assess players' coordination, agility, and balance. Determining the skill level of your players needs to be done during the first practice. Once you know what you are facing, you will be able to establish a schedule to improve their skills and eliminate any deficiencies they may have.

Once the actual games begin, the players' performances in the game will indicate additional areas you need to concentrate on. Always take a notebook and write down those skills the team does well and those it does not do as well. Set your practice schedules to work on the deficiencies you observed, making improvements on players' skills, tactics, and techniques.

To assess players, make sure you have a clipboard with a single sheet of paper with all of your players' names on it. You can list the different skills on one sheet of paper, or you can set up a separate sheet for each skill you want to observe. Take notes on each player as you observe them. You can use simple notes such as: "A" for advanced skills, "B" for basic skills, and "NI" for lacking the basic skills and needs improvement.

Using a sheet of paper, list the assessment drills across the top of the page and then list the names of the players down the left side of the page, as shown in Table 3.1. Draw lines to ensure you are able to put the comments next to the correct player. Take these notes as your players perform. Many players will want to see what you are writing and will try to look at the sheet of paper on the clipboard. By using a code system like the one described above, the players will be unable to determine what you are writing and how you are grading.

Table 3.1 Assessment List

	Cone Dribbling	Run to Goal	Fast Kick	2 vs. 2	Shoot on Goal	Throw-In	Chip
Name							
Name							
Name							
Name							

 NOTE: Many practice areas are open fields with no soccer goals. If you practice in an area like this, and you do not have access to a real soccer goal, you can simulate the left and right goalposts by using cones. Just place a cone on the ground, step off the distance of the opening of a real goal, and then place the other cone to represent the other goalpost. You now have a goal area where your players can shoot on the goal.

 Throughout this book, the symbols shown in Table 3.2 will be used.

Table 3.2

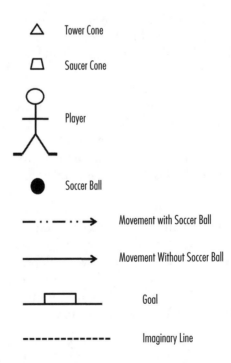

△	Tower Cone
▱	Saucer Cone
🯅	Player
●	Soccer Ball
– ·· — ·· →	Movement with Soccer Ball
⟶	Movement Without Soccer Ball
⊐	Goal
- - - - - - -	Imaginary Line

The following terms will also be used:

- **Skills:** These are movements required to play soccer. Some skills are dribbling, passing, shooting, and receiving.
- **Techniques:** Skills that enable a player to understand and participate in the game.
- **Tactics:** This term incorporates both the skill and technique to make an actual play or movement that is part of soccer.
- **Position play:** This is a controlled scrimmage. Rather than just playing, every time the ball is played it is for a designated reason. It might be to center the ball, for instance. After the play is over, the team returns to the kickoff and starts again. Position play involves repetitive drills designed to improve skill, technique, and tactics.

Initial Assessment

These assessment drills will enable you to get a comprehensive evaluation of your team. This is essential for all new teams and is also valuable for returning teams since most have new players. Evaluating all players at the beginning of each season will allow you to concentrate on the skills and techniques needed to develop your team.

NOTE: Each player needs shin guards. No player should ever participate in any practice or games without approved shin guards.

Straight Cone Dribbling   (Figure 3.1)

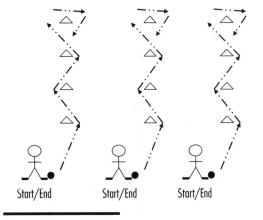

Figure 3.1
Straight Cone Dribbling

Purpose: This drill is used to evaluate dribbling skills as a player moves forward and directs the ball left and right around the cones.

Preparation: Place cones in a straight line with about two or three steps between each cone. Use at least four cones. The space between cones can be increased for older players and decreased for younger players, but normally two to three steps is a good distance. Place multiple rows of cones side by side so you can run multiple players simultaneously and don't have players standing around doing nothing for a long time.

Player needs: Each player needs to have his or her own ball.

Drill execution: Each player will dribble through the cones, going to the right side of one cone and then to the left side of the next cone. The player will continue to weave through the cones. When the player gets to the last cone, that player turns back and repeats the course from the opposite direction.

Coaching tips: While the players are dribbling through the cones, watch their foot action, balance, and coordination. Also look at their heads. They should not look only at the ball, and they should keep control of the ball by keeping it within a comfortable range where they can reach the ball at all times. They should be able to direct the ball right and left without stopping the ball.

1. Do the players have control and maintain control of the ball?

2. Is their movement fluid, or is every move a separate action?

3. How are they controlling the ball?

4. Are they using the inside of the foot or the outside of the foot? They have to keep the ball within their control area. Chances are, if they are only using the outside of their feet to redirect or push the ball, they will not have the ball in front of them and will lack control.

5. Do the players dribble while keeping their heads up to see the field?

6. Are they balanced as they move through the cones? The ball should stay in front of each player so he or she can maintain control of the ball. The player and the ball should move as one. Don't let the player kick the ball and then run to it.

Run to Goal   (Figure 3.2)

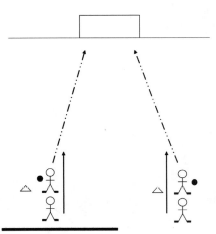

Figure 3.2
Run to Goal

Purpose: The object of this drill is for the player with the ball to dribble to the goal and shoot. The defender tries to get the ball away before that player can reach the goal. This drill shows a player's dribbling skills as well as the offensive and defensive skills of all of the players.

Preparation: Use a goal, or use cones to mark the perimeter of the goal. Place cones at midfield. Line up players in two lines so each line is just outside each goalpost at the end of the field. Break up the players into teams of two. If you have a goalkeeper, you can include that player in this drill.

Player needs: Each team of two players needs only one ball.

Drill execution: Place one player in front of the other. The front player has the ball. When you blow the whistle, the player with the ball starts dribbling toward the goal. As soon as the first player has taken a step, blow the whistle again for the second player to take off. The second player tries to reach the first player and gain possession of the ball by taking it away from the player that is dribbling toward the goal. After the two players have performed the drill, send them to the rear of the line and start with the next two players. When everyone has run the drill, switch and now let the original defender have the ball and send the offensive player to the defense.

Coaching tips: Players should be able to dribble and maintain speed. They must maintain control of the ball. They should be aware of where each defender is, even if the defender is behind them and they cannot see that player. Dribblers must keep their heads up to watch the field. If they watch only the ball, they will be unable to properly move to open space. The defender needs to get between the player and the goal and should switch to the inside of the offensive player. If the defender can reach the ball, he or she should either take control or side kick the ball away from the offensive player. When the offensive player reaches an open point, that player should shoot without hesitation or setting up the ball.

1. Watch for dribbling skills. Make sure the player with the ball doesn't kick and then run to the ball. A player must maintain control, even when running fast.

2. Observe the defender or the player chasing. Is that player moving to the inside of the player with the ball to force the offensive player to the outside of the goal area?

3. Watch the player with the ball. Is the player using the proper techniques for dribbling, control of the ball, shielding (if required), and shooting on goal?

4. Observe the player without the ball. Is this player using the proper techniques for moving goal-side and stripping the ball from the offensive player by either kicking it away or actually gaining control of the ball?

5. Is the player dribbling watching the ball and looking for openings on the field?

NOTE: Use this drill to see each player's speed, skills, agility, awareness, anticipation, and attitude.

Fast Kick   (Figure 3.3)

Figure 3.3
Fast Kick

Purpose: This drill evaluates your players' reflex actions.

Preparation: Divide your players into teams of two. Try to match the players in size and skill.

Player needs: Each team of two players needs a ball.

Drill execution: Have players stand, facing each other, and place the ball between them. The players need to be close enough to kick the ball. Have one player kick the ball. When the second player sees the player start to kick the ball, that player should also kick the ball. If the reflexes are good on both players, the kick will be blocked and the ball will stay between the two players. They will each hit the ball about the same time. Let one player start the kick for five times; then switch and let the other player start the kick. Repeat as necessary.

Coaching tips: Each player should be able to kick the ball at the same time. A player needs to watch the foot of the player kicking and move quickly to block the ball. Players should not be afraid, nor should they develop an attitude by bragging or getting depressed.

1. Watch each player. Is he or she using the laces of the shoes to make the kick?

2. Do the players anticipate the kick and move quickly to block it?

3. Watch how each player reacts. Is he or she afraid of getting hurt? Let each know that he or she can actually block the kick and avoid getting hurt.

NOTE: This drill allows you to check each player's reaction speed, awareness, skill, and attitude toward getting kicked.

2 vs. 2 Offense and Defense   (Figure 3.4)

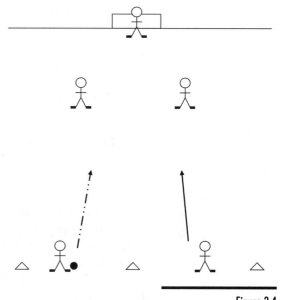

Purpose: This drill emphasizes teamwork, passing skills, and offensive and defensive skills.

Preparation: Use a goal or cones to mark the perimeter of the goal. Place cones at the midfield as a starting point for each player. The cones should be approximately 10 steps apart. Pick players in twos.

Player needs: The two players at the midfield point need one ball.

Drill execution: Place two players about 10 steps out from the goal. Their backs will be facing the goal and their fronts facing midfield. They are the defenders. Place two players with one ball at midfield. When you blow the whistle, the pair with the ball starts moving down the field. They will try to get past the two defenders by passing the ball to each other. A goal-keeper can be used during this drill. After the play is over, the two players playing offense stay and move to the defense while the two defenders move to the midfield to become offensive players.

Figure 3.4
2 vs. 2
Offense and Defense

Coaching tips: When you blow the whistle to start the drill, observe the offense and defense. The defensive players should move toward the offensive players. The offensive players should position themselves so they are close enough to pass. The player who doesn't have the ball should move to stay open. The player with the ball should keep the ball until challenged. This eliminates the opportunity for the defensive player to get the ball from a pass that is too early. The defensive players should stay positioned so their backs are to the goal, and they should move with the offensive players to intercept any pass.

1. Do the defenders just stand and wait, or do they move toward the ball? They should move.

2. Do the offensive players move so they can place themselves two on one against one of the defenders?

3. Does the offensive player that is off the ball move so the player with the ball can pass to him or her when the defensive player gets within two steps?

4. Does the offensive player with the ball hold the ball until the very last moment and then pass after the defensive player has committed?

5. Do the defensive players move to cut the angle of the pass and also ensure each offensive player is covered?

6. When one of the offensive players has an opening, does that player shoot on goal?

7. Does the goalkeeper move to guard the goal as the ball switches around the field?

NOTE: This drill will tell you a lot about your players. The player with the ball should hold the ball until challenged and then pass when the defender is approximately two steps away. This will keep that defender from capturing the ball or intercepting the pass. The second offensive player, the one off the ball, should be moving to open space to receive the pass. The defenders should stay between the player with the ball and the goal to eliminate the opportunity to shoot on goal. The defender off the ball should move with the offensive player off the ball to eliminate the pass to that player. The goalkeeper's movement should be constant. If an offensive player gets open and has the opportunity, that player should shoot on goal without hesitation.

Shooting on Goal (Figure 3.5)

Purpose: This drill is a combination of dribbling and the ability to move to open spaces.

Preparation: Use a goal or cones to mark the perimeter of the goal. Place three players at midfield and all other players between the three players at midfield and the goal. Place cones behind the players who are standing between midfield and the goal. They cannot leave the cones. Also, place cones five steps from the goal.

Player needs: Each of the players at midfield needs a ball. The remaining players will not be moving. They will stand still so the player with the ball has to dribble around them.

Drill execution: Place the players that are standing between midfield and the goal so there is no direct path to the goal. These players will not move while the player from midfield is dribbling through them. When the player with the ball gets

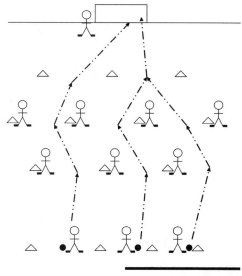

Figure 3.5
Shooting on Goal

through the standing players and reaches the shooting cones nearest the goal, he or she must shoot on goal at that point.

    The player who dribbles through the other players and shoots on goal then goes and replaces one of the standing players. The standing player who was replaced gets the ball and goes to midfield. As soon as a player has shot the ball and moved to replace a player, start the next player from midfield. The players can take multiple routes between the players. Let them decide which route to take.

Coaching tips: Watch the player with the ball. This player should move to open space between the standing players. He or she should shoot quickly without any hesitation. The ball should be kicked away from the goalkeeper and into the side of the goal. The kick should be hard and direct.

1. Does the player with the ball move to open space between the standing players?

2. When the player gets to the shooting cone, does that player shoot or take time to set up the ball?

3. Does the shooter place the ball away from the goalkeeper or if there is no goalkeeper in the side of the goal?

4. Does the shooter use the laces of his or her shoe when taking the shot?

5. Is the kick hard or soft?

Throw-In   (Figure 3.6)

Purpose: Long throw-ins require upper body strength, something very few young players have. The most important aspect of a throw-in is accuracy, and proper technique is essential for accuracy.

Preparation: Set up cones to form two horizontal lines approximately 5 to 10 steps apart.

Player needs: One ball is required for every two players.

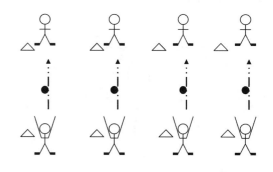

Figure 3.6
Throw-In

Drill execution: Place half your players on one line of cones and the other half on the cones that are parallel to the first set of players. The player with the ball will throw the ball to the player opposite him or her. The player receiving the ball can use any technique to gather the ball except catching it with his or her hands. Start by throwing to the feet of the opposite player and then move to the head. If the ball is not accurate, see if the player receiving the ball moves to center on the ball and then uses the proper technique for receiving the ball, i.e., thighs, chest, and so on. After the player collects the ball, he or she picks it up and throws it back to the opposite player using the proper throw-in technique.

Coaching tips: Proper throw-ins are essential to maintain control of the ball.

1. Are the hands evenly spaced and to the rear and side of the ball?

2. Is the ball placed at the rear of the head and then brought forward evenly?

3. Is the spin on the ball forward? If the ball has a sideward spin, the player is using one hand more than the other.

4. Does the player keep both feet on the ground when making the throw?

5. Does the player receiving the ball trap the ball with a foot? Use his or her head properly to head the ball? Use chest or thighs to trap the ball?

NOTE: This simple drill will tell you a lot about each player's throwing in and receiving skills.

Chip (Figure 3.7)

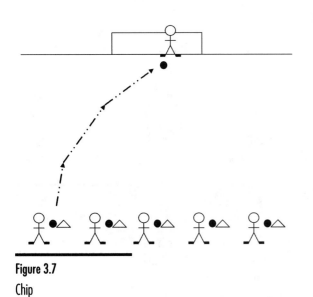

Figure 3.7
Chip

Purpose: The ability to chip, or lift the ball off the ground, is a necessity. This skill is used during a corner kick, during play when the ball needs to be lifted over the defense, during direct and indirect penalty kicks, when moving the ball out of the defense, and many other times during a game. Some players may already have the ability while others have to be trained. You need to know which players can already do the chip as you train the others.

Preparation: Use a goal or cones to mark the perimeter of the goal. Set up a line of cones at the edge of the penalty box or approximately 18 steps. The chips the players are performing will be kicked toward the goal. Place your goalkeeper in the goal.

Player needs: Each player needs a ball.

Drill execution: This drill is done two separate ways. The first is a kick with the ball sitting still. Have each player place the ball on the ground near the cone and then run at and kick the ball toward the goal. After each player has done this twice and you have noted who can and cannot do this, move the players back and have them dribble to the cone and chip the ball while on the run. After the kick, each player collects the ball and returns to the line. If the goalkeeper got the ball, the goalkeeper can return the ball to the player by rolling it or throwing it to the outside of the goal area.

Coaching tips: Make sure each player is watching the ball when kicking it. A player's leg should go completely through the ball and not stop when the foot connects with the ball.

1. Is the plant foot pointing in the direction of the kick?

2. Does the player kick through the ball rather than kicking just the ball?

3. Does the player have the toe down and use the laces of his or her shoe to get underneath the ball?

NOTE: This drill will give you an idea of each player's kicking ability, attitude, and enthusiasm.

Warm-Up, Stretch, and Ball Control Drills

Warm-up and stretch drills are a must for every practice and game. Many coaches mistakenly believe that players already have gotten exercise at school or during the day. While they may have gotten some exercise, proper warm-up and stretch drills have a dual purpose. These drills allow players to warm up and stretch their muscles, decreasing the possibility of injury, and also develop necessary soccer skills and muscle development. Adding some ball control drills helps to get the players up to the proper playing condition faster.

You can vary the type of warm-up drills you do, but you will find that if you select a set of drills and stick to them your players will become comfortable with them and also develop skills and muscles.

Many coaches just do a warm-up, but adding stretching helps players develop faster. You can incorporate many different moves in each of the drills. You are only limited by your imagination.

Using these warm-up, stretch, and ball control drills is a great way to start each practice. Having players practice the same thing builds teamwork and develops the skills and muscles needed to become the best soccer players possible.

Warm-Up

The following warm-up drills are essential to ensure your players decrease the chance for injuries and build the necessary strengths needed in the game of soccer. Each warm-up is designed to provide strength, cardiovascular endurance, and agility.

Slow Run   (Figures 4.1 and 4.2)

Purpose: The slow run is important to loosen up the muscles and to help develop cardiovascular endurance. If you are practicing on a field that does not have lines marked out, set cones to mark the corners of the slow run so the players know where to turn. Figure 4.1 shows a run path. If you have a young team, you may want to use half of the field; for older teams, use the whole field.

Preparation: Place the players in twos, one beside the other. (See Figure 4.2.) Keep approximately two to three steps between each player to their front and back.

Player needs: None

Drill execution: Have the players do a slow jog around the field. Running in formation helps develop teamwork. It puts players together as a team with all doing the same thing.

Coaching tips: Remember, kids want to run fast but need to learn that a slow jog is better to warm up. A fast run can cause injuries and must be avoided.

1. Are your players staying in formation? If not you may have to call cadence such as, left . . left . . . left . . . right . . . left. This gets everyone in step and keeps them working as a team.

2. Are they doing a slow jog or are they trying to run? Keep them slow.

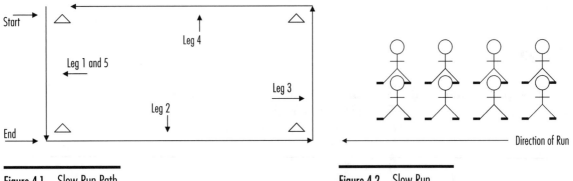

Figure 4.1   Slow Run Path

Figure 4.2   Slow Run

Knee Lift   (Figure 4.3)

Purpose: The following are different movements you can add to the slow run. All are good for developing strength, and most are movements used in game play.

Preparation: Keep the players in the twos formation and doing a slow jog.

Player needs: None

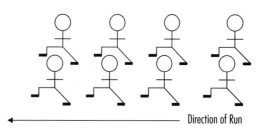

Direction of Run

Figure 4.3
Knee Lift

Drill execution: When the players reach the first corner and make the turn, have them lift their legs as they run. The knees should come up to at least their waists, and players will look like they are prancing. The pace of the run remains the same as the slow run.

Coaching tips: If your players go to a high school or above game they will see the players doing leg lifts. This is an important part of limbering up.

1. Are the players lifting their legs so the knee is straight away from the waist?

2. Are your players able to maintain the jog while lifting their legs?

Backward Run   (Figure 4.4)

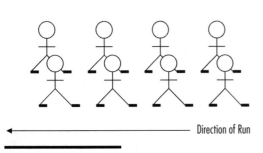

←——————————————————— Direction of Run

Figure 4.4
Backward Run

Purpose: This movement is one that the players will use on the field during a game. There will be many times when the players have to move backward as their opponents approach. Older players can do this with little or no difficulty, but younger players may find it hard at the beginning.

Preparation: After the players have completed the section doing the leg lift, have them turn around so they are running backward. Ensure the players are separated two to three steps so they don't run into other players.

Player needs: None

Drill execution: While running backward, have players concentrate on the player directly in front to keep their own direction and distance.

Coaching tips: You may have to put your young players outside of a formation to learn to run backward without falling; once they can maintain balance when running backward, get them back in formation.

1. Are the players able to run backward without falling?

2. Are the players able to stay in their running formation? Keep them together in the side-by-side formation.

3. Are they still maintaining the same slow run? Speed is not important, proper execution is important.

Side Step   (Figure 4.5)

Purpose: Knowing the proper way to sidestep, or move sideways without having your feet cross over each other, is also essential during the game.

Preparation: After completing the backward run, have the players switch to the side step. Have them turn so they are facing the inside of the field and are looking at you.

Player needs: None

Drill execution: When moving sideways, the feet should come together and then the lead foot moves away again, followed by the back foot coming to the lead foot.

Coaching tips: If the players step over their legs rather than side-to-side they will not be able to keep their balance or move quickly in the opposite direction if needed.

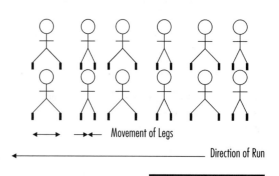

Movement of Legs

Direction of Run

Figure 4.5
Side Step

1. Did the players all turn facing to the inside of the field?

2. Are the players bringing their feet together and not stepping over? It is essential that the players learn to sidestep rather than stepping over their other foot. This will ensure balance and speed.

Rear Leg Lift (Figure 4.6)

————————————— Direction of Run

Figure 4.6
Rear Leg Lift

Purpose: While running the fifth and last leg of the run, have players kick their legs up behind them. If they are doing the run properly, the heels of their shoes should come up and touch their rear ends. This limbers up and stretches their legs and muscles.

Preparation: Have the players turn from the side step so they are again facing forward and in the formation.

Player needs: None

Drill execution: While performing the slow jog, have the players kick their legs backward until the heels of their shoes are touching their rear end. Continue the jog while they perform the rear leg lift.

Coaching tips: This is another drill that may seem dumb but is very important for stretching the muscles and providing balance and agility.

1. Is each player lifting their legs until they make contact with their rear end?

2. Are the players continuing to stay in formation and moving forward?

Stretches

Stretches have a dual purpose. First they allow players to stretch their muscles before play, but stretches also develop the muscles needed during the game. Again, there are many different drills that can be used. The drills listed here are good for stretching and muscle development.

Center Stretch   (Figure 4.7)

Purpose: This simple stretch is intended to stretch the muscles before going into the muscle development drills.

Preparation: Place the players in a circle so they are facing you. You will be in the center of the circle. Ensure there is space between the players to allow them to step right and left.

Player needs: None

Drill execution: These stretches need to be done in a static movement. Do not allow players to bounce up and down or reach back and forth. When doing the drill, have them reach out and hold the position for a count of at least five. You can also do these on a count of 10. At the end of each drill count tell them to release. Have players place their legs to the right and the left of their bodies. Then have them bend forward, keeping their legs straight. They will touch the ground in between their legs and as far behind as possible.

Coaching tips: Players want to bounce up and down but can pull muscles if they do. A simple stretch and hold is important.

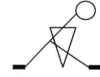

Figure 4.7
Center Stretch

1. Are the players touching the ground with their hands?

2. Are they holding in a static position? Bouncing can cause injuries.

3. Are you able to turn freely to see all of the players?

Right and Left Stretch   (Figure 4.8)

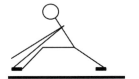 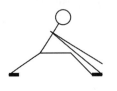

Figure 4.8
Right and Left Stretch

Purpose: Use this drill to stretch the muscles before going into the development drills. Whether stretching to the right or left, the same principles and moves are used.

Preparation: Keep the players in a circle facing inward toward you in the center of the circle.

Player needs: None

Drill execution: To start the stretch, take one leg, right or left, and have the player step away from his or her body with foot pointing outward. That leg will be bent. The back leg needs to be straight with the foot pointing toward the other foot. Have the player reach down and touch the lead foot, which is the one with the leg bent. Have players hold this stretch until you finish the count and tell them to release. After the release, have them turn to the other side and repeat the action doing the same movement using their other legs.

Coaching tips: Again stretch and hold is important. Make sure they stretch out, and don't let them hold back by just leaning on their leg.

1. Are the players stretching out as far as they can?

2. Are they holding their stretch and not bouncing?

3. Do you have the players stretching in the same direction? It is important to have the players do everything together and the same. This builds working as a team.

Knee Touch Stretch   (Figure 4.9)

Purpose: This is the first muscle development drill and builds leg
strength.

Preparation: Have the player place the soccer ball to the right side,
against the right foot, while standing up straight with both
feet together.

Player needs: One soccer ball per person.

Drill execution: Have the player lift and bend the right leg and hold
it against his or her rear end. Then while standing on one leg
(left leg) have the player lower the body until the right knee
touches the ball. After touching the ball, the player lifts back
up. Start with five touches with each leg.

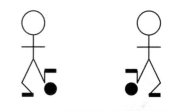

Figure 4.9
Knee Touch Stretch

All of the movement and strength will be on the left leg, which is low-
ering and lifting the player. After the player has touched the ball five times
with the knee, have the player step to the other side of the ball and lower
and rise using the right leg, touching the ball with the left knee.

To help players keep their balance, they will have to look out in front
of them at least three feet. Looking straight down at the ball will cause
them to lose their balance. This is a great drill to develop the leg muscles
used in soccer.

Coaching tips: This drill develops the leg strength the players need. As they
become proficient and stronger you will be able to see the difference in
their play on the field.

1. Is each player able to lower and raise him- or herself just using one leg?
    If not, this is okay, because the player will eventually be able to perform
    the drill. When first starting keep the repetitions low and increase the
    number as each builds strength.

2. Are the players able to maintain their balance? If not, have them look
    out away from their body. Don't let them look straight down.

3. Are the players holding their leg tight against their body? If not, have
    them hold their leg rather than just let it stick out in the back.

Jump the Ball   (Figure 4.10)

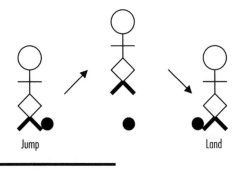

Jump   Land

Figure 4.10
Jump the Ball

Purpose: This is another good drill for muscle development. This drill also helps players learn to jump with balance.

Preparation: Have players place the ball beside the right or left foot while standing straight up. They should have their feet together.

Player needs: Each player needs their own ball.

Drill execution: While standing next to the soccer ball have each player use their toes to propel themselves up and over the ball. Make sure they keep their ankles together and do not spread their feet apart. They will be jumping sideways over the ball. They should do 10 jumps, 5 each way.

When they first start doing this drill, players may land on the ball and fall. They may also jump and stop before jumping again. Keep them moving until they are able to jump over the ball sideways without stopping between jumps. Eventually they will be able to jump back and forth in a fluid movement. After each player has made the jumps from side-to-side, repeat the drill by placing the ball on the ground in front of each player and having them jump over the ball front-to-back. When first starting this front-to-back jump, the players will often fall when jumping backward. Emphasize proper jumping by using their toes to propel them higher and farther.

Coaching tips: Jumping to head the ball is a must. This builds the leg strength and technique they need to properly jump. This will increase the height of their jump.

1. Are the players using their toes to jump? Don't allow them to jump flat-footed.

2. Are they keeping their feet together as they jump? Don't let them spread their feet; their shoes should be touching.

3. Do the players do the drill in a smooth motion? Don't let them stop or pause after each jump.

Karaoke (Figures 4.11 and 4.12)

Purpose: Karaoke is a ball control, balance, and agility drill that is best done during the warm-up period of each practice. Doing this drill helps a player move the ball, develop touch on the ball, and develop good balance. This is a good drill for soccer development.

Be patient because players will not grasp this drill immediately. Work with them to strike the ball and move the ball in a straight line, switching feet with every new touch on the ball. They will eventually be able to fluidly move the ball down the field in a straight line without stopping.

Preparation: To do this drill the player will step over the ball with one foot and then push the ball with the instep of the other foot. To start, place the ball on the ground in front of the player. Have each player stand directly behind the ball with both feet approximately at shoulder width.

Start with the ball in front of the player.

Step over the ball with the left foot.

Strike the ball with the instep of the right foot.

Figure 4.11
Karaoke, Step Left

Start with the ball in front of the player.

Step over the ball with the right foot.

Strike the ball with the instep of the left foot.

Figure 4.12
Karaoke, Step Right

Player needs: Each player needs his or her own ball.

Drill execution: With the ball in front, have the player step over the ball with the left foot. The left foot will now be on the right side of the ball. The player will then swing the right foot under the left leg and into the ball, kicking it with the instep of the right foot. This will propel the ball forward.

The next touch is just the reverse. Have the player step over the ball with the right foot. The right foot will now be on the left side of the ball. The player will then swing the left foot under the right leg and into the ball, kicking it with the instep of the left foot.

The foot that touches the ball will always be the back foot. The front foot will be the one that steps over the ball to the opposite side. After they have done this drill a few times, players will be able to move the ball and keep their balance. If you have younger players, have them do the karaoke from the center line to the end line and back. If you have older players, they can go from end line to end line.

Coaching tips: This is seldom if ever used in a game, but it is an ideal drill to gain confidence, agility, and balance. They also learn control of the ball.

1. Are the players pushing or kicking the ball with their back foot?

2. Are they twisting sideways to maintain balance?

3. Are they moving the ball forward in a straight line?

4. Does each player move forward and switch direction with each kick?

Ball Roll Over, Forward (Figure 4.13)

Purpose: In this ball control drill, the player moves the ball by rolling a foot across the top of the ball. This technique is used in situations where the player needs to move the ball left to right while maintaining close control. This drill is rolling the ball forward from one end of the field to the other, using the right foot one way down the field and the left foot on the return.

Right Foot

Left Foot

Figure 4.13
Ball Roll Over, Forward

Preparation: Put the players in a line, side by side across the field. Have each player place the ball to the right side. Ensure there are at least two to three steps of separation between the players.

Player needs: Each player needs his or her own ball.

Drill execution: Using the right foot, the player will move it over the ball from the back to the front, causing the ball to roll forward. The player does not kick the ball, but gently moves the foot across the top of the ball from the top back to the top front. As the ball moves down the field, the player continues to follow it and keeps it moving by rolling the foot over the ball. The ball should stay in continuous motion. As the player returns down the field, have him or her use the left foot to roll the ball.

Coaching tips: This enables each player to learn control and balance using both feet. This is a must when in close contact with the opposing player. Learning this allows your player to move and maintain control of the ball until he or she can pass or move away.

1. Are the players rolling the ball? Do not let them kick the ball because this drill aims to develop touch and control on the ball.

2. Are the players keeping the ball moving straight down the field, or are they moving side to side? Emphasize keeping the ball rolling straight.

3. Do the players maintain balance and continuous motion forward?

Ball Roll Over, Forward and Back   (Figure 4.14)

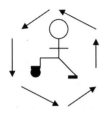

Counterclockwise Roll, Forward

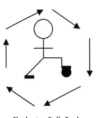

Clockwise Roll, Back

Figure 4.14
Ball Roll Over,
Forward and Back

Purpose: This drill teaches the player to control the ball by using a rollover in order to move the ball forward and backward. This is very helpful when shielding the ball or moving the ball to get into position to pass. This drill involves controlling the ball in a forward and backward motion by rolling the ball using the right foot one complete 360-degree turn in a counterclockwise direction and then stopping the ball and rolling it one complete 360-degree turn in the clockwise direction.

Preparation: Have the player place the ball in front. Make sure each player is separated so he or she can make a 360-degree turn.

Player needs: Each player needs to have his or her own ball.

Drill execution: With the ball in front of them and using the right foot, roll the ball forward by going in the counterclockwise direction. The player will turn a full circle by rolling the ball. When back to the starting position, the player stops and rolls the ball backward using the same foot but now turning in a clockwise direction. After doing this a few times, have the player switch to the left foot and repeat the action. Make sure each player rolls the ball just enough to maintain control and turn as he or she rolls the ball.

Coaching tips: The better your players can do this, the better they will be able to maintain ball control during the game. The player that stops the ball rather than keeping it moving is the player that is about to lose the ball.

1. Is each player able to maintain control of the ball with both feet?

2. Are the players moving in a fluid motion?

3. Are the players maintaining their balance?

CHAPTER 5

Cooldown

After a practice in which you have run many drills and the players have worked hard, it is important to let them slow down and cool off. This time is normally called the cooldown period. Many coaches use a slow run or a jog as the cooldown. This is a great way to slow things down, but it does not develop any soccer skills. Most coaches are limited in the time they have to practice, so everything you do in your practice schedule should directly relate to building soccer skills. It makes the practices more efficient.

Using drills that allow the players to calm down and relax while at the same time hone their skills will put you ahead of your competition. The following are drills that can be used in practice but are ideal for cooldown. To give you time to set up the drill areas, give the team a water break. By the time they have finished, you should be ready to do the cooldown drill. To keep the cooldown period interesting, rotate the drills you use.

Penalty Kick (Figure 5.1)

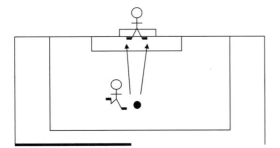

Figure 5.1
Penalty Kick

Purpose: The penalty kick is not a play used often on the soccer field, but you do need to know who can and who cannot perform it. This kick is done with the ball stationary and will enable players to develop a more accurate kick.

Preparation: Use a goal or cones to mark the perimeter of the goal and a mark for the penalty mark. You can use a tower cone or a saucer cone to identify the penalty mark. Set one or two cones inside each side goalpost. These cones are the target the players will shoot for. If you have a goalkeeper, you can use that player.

Player needs: Each player will need his or her own ball.

Drill execution: Place the goalkeeper in the goal area. Line up the players outside the penalty box. Have one player at a time enter the penalty box and place the ball on the penalty mark. That player will shoot on goal. The goalkeeper needs to follow the rules of a penalty kick by staying on the goal line and not moving until the ball is kicked. If players miss the goal, they must go get their balls.

Coaching tips: Although penalty kicks are seldom done, when it is necessary, you must know who can and cannot make the kick. This is often the difference in winning and losing. Accuracy is a must.

1. Make sure your players kick the ball toward the cones that you placed just inside the goalposts. It is important the player kicks away from the goalkeeper.

2. Watch that your players do not use their toes to kick. They can use a kick or a pass to place the ball.

3. Be aware that the players waiting to kick will be talking. So if you have a point to make you will first have to get their attention. Since this is a cooldown period, let your players relax.

Corner Kick   (Figure 5.2)

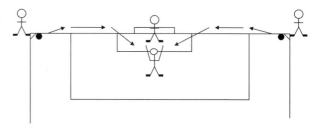

Purpose: There will be quite a few opportunities in a game to do a corner kick. Some of your players will be able to lift the ball better than others. This is a chance to practice the kick and find out who is the best. It will also develop the players that are weak.

Preparation: Use a goal or cones to mark the perimeter of the goal. Place a cone to mark each corner flag. Divide the players so half of the team is at each corner flag.

Figure 5.2
Corner Kick

Player needs: Each player needs to have a ball.

Drill execution: Start by having one of the players on each side place the ball in the quarter circle. Pick one to start the kick. Place the goalkeeper in the goal. You as the coach need to stand in front of the goal about five steps out. Raise your hands in the air. This is where the players need to try to kick the ball.

If the goalkeeper catches the ball, he or she should roll it to the opposite side from the kick and back to the next player waiting. If the ball goes over to the other side, let it go and have a player on that side pick it up. This will save the players having to chase the ball, which means you can get more kicks in a shorter time.

Coaching tips: On a corner kick, distance and accuracy are important.

1. Make sure players do not use their toes to kick the ball.

2. Emphasize distance and accuracy.

3. Look for the players that are the most consistent in their kicks.

Chip to Goal   (Figure 5.3)

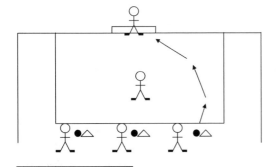

Figure 5.3
Chip to Goal

Purpose: Passing on the ground is an important skill in soccer, but so is the ability to be able to chip the ball into the air and over the heads of other players. This is a drill where the players can learn touch on the ball and also accuracy. It is another good drill for the cooldown period because the players are static and not running.

Preparation: Use a goal or cones to mark the perimeter of the goal. With the cones, mark three or four spots just outside of the penalty box.

Player needs: Each player needs a ball.

Drill execution: Line up the players in three or four lines behind the cones that are lined up just outside the penalty box. If you have fewer players, you will need fewer lines. The more players you have, the more lines you need. Put your goalkeeper in the goal to catch the balls. You will stand halfway between the players kicking the ball and the goal. The players need to kick the ball over your head. The goalkeeper can roll or throw the ball back out to the players kicking the ball.

Coaching tips: A chip is a very effective tool in soccer. The ability to lift the ball over opponents as a pass or a shot is a must.

1. Watch that players do not use their toes to kick the ball.

2. Have players kick the ball below the center of the ball and on the back side.

3. Make sure players follow through on the ball to get the proper lift. All kicks should be through the ball. Never stop the kick when hitting the ball.

4. Watch to make sure each player places the plant foot just behind and to the side of the ball rather than even with the ball.

5. Take notice of the players who are able to lift the ball. If players aren't lifting the ball, show them the proper way to do a chip.

6. Make sure the player is able to lift the ball and accurately place it in the goal area.

Throw-In to Goal (Figure 5.4)

Purpose: This drill is done exactly like the chip to goal drill except players throw the ball over the head of the coach and into the goal. Younger teams can move closer to the goal.

Preparation: Use a goal or cones to mark the perimeter of the goal. Use cones to mark three or four spots just outside of the penalty box.

Player needs: Each player needs a ball.

Drill execution: Line up the players in three or four lines behind the cones that are just beyond the outer edge of the penalty box. If you have fewer players, you will need fewer lines. The more players you have, the more lines you need. Put your goalkeeper in the goal to catch the balls. You will stand halfway between the players throwing the ball and the goal. The players need to try to throw the ball over your head. The goalkeeper can roll or throw the ball back out to the players doing the throw-in.

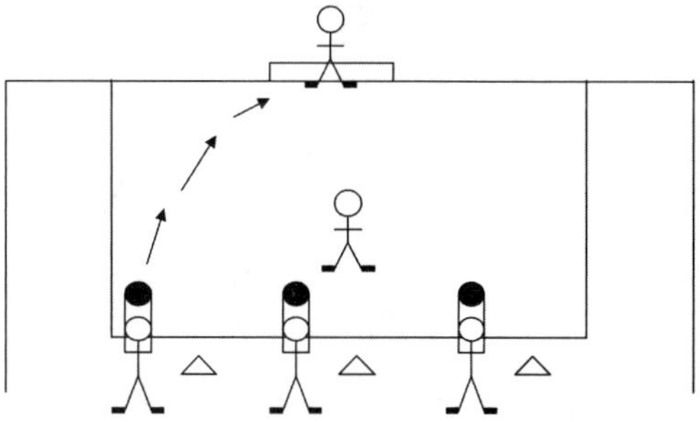

Figure 5.4
Throw-In to Goal

Coaching tips: Controlling the throw of the ball is important. Accuracy of the throw is the difference between whether you maintain control of the ball or lose the ball to the other team.

1. Watch that the players do not lift their feet from the ground when they throw the ball.

2. Have the players place their hands on the ball on the sides and just to the rear of center. Their hands should form the letter W.

3. See that players stand and throw or take a few steps and throw. Either way the feet must stay in contact with the ground.

4. Take notice of the players who are able to properly throw the ball. If players aren't throwing the ball correctly, show them the proper way to do a throw-in.

5. Make sure players are able to throw the ball into the air and accurately place it in the goal area.

Pass Relay in Teams (Figure 5.5)

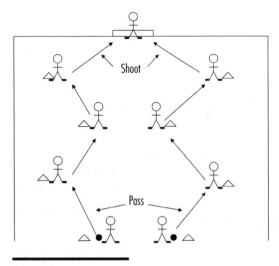

Figure 5.5
Pass Relay in Teams

Purpose: This is another static drill that develops the skills needed for game situations. Passing is important, and this drill not only promotes accurate passing but also receiving and shooting. It is done as a competition between teams of players.

Preparation: Use a goal or cones to mark the perimeter of the goal. Place cones down the field leaving about 10 steps between each cone. You will need a separate set of cones for each team. Do not use any more than five players on a team. Put your goalkeeper in the goal.

Player needs: Each team needs one ball.

Drill execution: Blow the whistle to start play. The first player in each line passes to the next player in line. This continues until the ball reaches the last player. The last player then shoots on goal. No players can be skipped. The first team to have the ball reach the goalkeeper wins the race.

After the shot, have each player rotate. The player shooting goes to the back of the line to start the passing on the next competition. Everyone else moves up one spot. Continue this until every player has shot. At that point you will have a winning team. You can repeat the drill if time permits.

Coaching tips: This drill is fun, yet it is important because the players learn very quickly that accuracy of their pass is important. They can't win with bad passes. This will also becomes evident in the games.

1. Watch the passes to make sure players are using the insteps of the feet.

2. Make sure passes go to the next player; accuracy is a must.

3. Observe how the players receive the ball, turn, and pass to the next player in line.

4. Be sure that when a player shoots, he or she turns and shoots — not dribbles. This is a timed game, and fewer touches on the ball actually speed up the play.

Drop Ball   (Figure 5.6)

Purpose: This is a near static drill that develops timing. The drop ball is seldom used in a game but is something the players should know.

Preparation: Split the players into teams of three.

Player needs: You need one ball per three players.

Drill execution: Have two players face each other. The third player will drop the ball between the other two players. Each player should try to kick the ball. Run this drill five times, and then change players. The player dropping the ball becomes a kicker, and one of the kickers drops the ball. Rotate until everyone has kicked the ball and everyone has dropped the ball.

Coaching tips: This is another part of the game that is seldom used, but your players need to know how to win control of the ball during a drop ball situation. This will also give you a good idea of each player's ability to react quickly.

Figure 5.6
Drop Ball

1. Make sure your players watch the ball. They should anticipate but not kick until the ball reaches the ground.

2. Check the reaction time of each player.

3. Make sure players don't use their hands to push back other players.

Problems and Solutions

Have you ever had a problem that you didn't know how to solve? Many coaches face this dilemma. They see what their team is doing wrong but do not know what to do to correct the problem. This chapter helps you identify the problem your team is having and then correct it with drills.

This chapter is set up in two distinct categories. The first includes "Problem" statements. These are the common problems each coach faces. Scan through the chapter until you find the specific problem statement your team is experiencing. Directly below the "Problem" will be the heading "Solution." The "Solution" is a group of drills that you can use to eliminate the deficiency.

The drills are specified by number, for example, Drill 9.1. The first number denotes the chapter, and the second number identifies the drill within that chapter. Therefore, Drill 9.1 is in Chapter 9 and is the first drill in that chapter. Similarly, Drill 9.5 is also in Chapter 9 but is the fifth drill. So, select your problem, read through the solution(s) listed, and then locate the drill for detailed instructions on how to implement it.

To make it easier to find the specific deficiency you need to correct, the main thrust of the problem is highlighted in each "Problem" statement.

Most of the time coaches will see players' deficiencies during practice. However, sometimes deficiencies only become apparent during a game. When deficiencies do appear in a game, they are usually amplified, causing the team to make mistakes and sometimes lose because of those mistakes.

Often the problems are caused by a lack of confidence by individual players. They don't know what they are doing and as a result don't trust their own ability. If they don't feel they are in control or can control the situation they won't try. This can manifest itself into many different problems. The more you work on individual skills, the more confidence your players will gain and the better they will play. When they know what to do in a situation, they will do it—or at least try to do it.

Many times you will find your players have the basic skills but are unable to translate them into the actual technique or tactic required on the field of play. It is a matter of learning the required skill and gaining knowledge of what has to be done at that specific time. These skills and knowledge can be learned through practice drills.

Problem

On the practice field my *players are out of control* and just want to run around and play.

Solution

This is an area that comes up often, generally for the same reasons.

1. You have to be the authority figure. You are the coach, not the players' best friend. Do not play soccer with the team during the practice. Oversee and supervise the actions of your players.
2. Your practices must be consistent. You should have a warm-up period; a main emphasis section, or sections, with drills designed to improve a deficient area; a conditioning period; and a cooldown period. Not being prepared and having the players stand around just invites the players to focus their attention on something other than soccer.
3. Players are looking for two things: an authority figure and to have fun. If your practices are not more fun than TV or video games, you are doing your practices wrong.
4. Use drills that are age and skill appropriate, and make them into fun games. The players will play games and never realize they are learning. Many of the drills in this book are fun, but they are teaching the players to properly perform on the soccer field. Get your players involved in the drills. They will have fun, they will learn, and they won't have time to do other things. They will want to be part of the fun the other players are having.
5. You don't have to be the villain; you just have to be in control and prepared.

Problem

My *players do not challenge the ball*. They are afraid of getting hit with the ball, so they stop and allow the other player to kick the ball.

Solution

There are a few different things that can cause this problem. First, the players might actually be afraid of the ball, but most likely they don't feel like they can get the ball. They would rather stay back and wait until the ball comes to them.

If a player is afraid of the ball, his or her actions will easily tell you. The player will run away from the ball, duck a ball that should be headed or trapped, jump and turn a back to the ball, or just move around the field so he or she is never in a position to be challenged. Often you will find out fear of the ball is less an issue for these players than their lack of confidence in their own ability to gain or maintain control of the situation. Since they don't feel confident, they avoid the situation. There are ways to stop this.

1. First of all, show the players that when they are close to the other player the ball has less room to travel and will hurt less if hit with it. This is only true if players are very close so that the trajectory of the ball will strike them in the knees or below.
2. Put your players in controlled situations where they can play soccer but not get hurt. They will learn that they can control the situation. There are many drills where this can be done. The following drills are good for the whole team and will improve players' performance, allow them to gain confidence, and, as a result, eliminate the factor that often manifests itself as a fear of the ball.

Offense and Defense Drills

- **Drill 12.1: Back and Forth to the Goal.** This drill places each player in a situation to play offense and defense.
- **Drill 12.5: Throw and Move.** This drill pits one player against another. Each player can switch from offense to defense. Play starts when a player wins the ball. This is also a good aggression development drill.
- **Drill 12.6: Throw and Turn.** This drill teaches the defense how to move to the ball and turn the ball. It teaches the offense how to capture the ball before the defense can turn the ball.
- **Drill 12.8: Through the Box.** This drill requires a player to go through several levels of defense before he or she can shoot on goal.

The second and most common reason players appear afraid of the ball is that most players are more comfortable with offense than with defense. Offense requires the player to move forward by dribbling to make moves to get past the defender, and to dribble or shoot. Defense requires challenging another player, getting into a confrontation, and taking the ball away from the other player. Confronting another player is something many players have to learn.

Teach all of your players both offensive moves as well as defensive moves. Don't just divide your team and practice offense with some and defense with others. All players must be on offense when your team has the ball, and all players must be on defense when the opposing team has the ball. All of your players should be able to play both ways.

1. Use the many different drills that combine defense and offense. Switching your players to offense and then to defense requires everyone to do both. Try to place your weaker players together, and likewise, your stronger players together. This will allow them to compete at their own levels and gain confidence and skill as they play.
2. Start with simple drills where the offense has the advantage, and then as the team improves, add more defense. This will increase the challenge level of your players and will require them to become more proficient with their offensive skills.

Dribbling Drills

- **Drill 8.4: Change Speed Dribbling.** This drill teaches players how to vary their speed while dribbling—a necessity for playing soccer.
- **Drill 8.5: Step Over Right/Left Dribbling.** This drill teaches players how to move the ball left and right while faking out the defense.
- **Drill 8.6: Fake Kick Dribbling.** This is a fake kick done while dribbling. This often freezes the defender, allowing the offensive player to move around that defender.
- **Drill 8.7: Turn and Dribble.** This drill teaches players how to reverse a ball that is coming straight at them from the front.

Passing Drills

- **Drill 9.4: Rock 'Em Sock 'Em Passing.** This drill is great to teach players when to pass. Many players hold the ball too long or pass before it's appropriate. This drill teaches timing and the necessity for accuracy in the pass.
- **Drill 9.5: Wall Pass.** The wall pass is a very effective method for moving around your opponent while maintaining control of the ball. This drill teaches the basics of working with a teammate to move past an opponent.
- **Drill 9.6: Pass Between Cones.** This drill is good because it teaches the short pass and also passing and receiving with both feet.
- **Drill 9.7: Drop Pass.** This drill teaches players how to work together to lay off a pass to another player moving in the opposite direction.

- **Drill 9.8: Reverse Pass.** This pass teaches players to be able to reverse the ball while on a full run.
- **Drill 9.9: Reverse Pass Team Competition.** This drill is a team activity that teaches the reverse pass, balance, coordination, and teamwork.
- **Drill 9.10: Pass Through Legs.** The ability to pass to the feet of another player is a must in soccer. This drill teaches the player the proper place to pass and how to receive by going to the ball.

Offense and Defense Drills
- **Drill 12.1: Back and Forth to the Goal.** This drill places each player in a situation to play offense and defense.
- **Drill 12.2: Two on One.** This drill teaches players how to get the defense to commit, when to pass, and how to move to open space.
- **Drill 12.3: Two on Two.** This drill teaches players, offense and defense, to play as a team. It also requires the offensive players to move to keep the defense in a moving or chase position.
- **Drill 12.4: Three on Three.** This drill is as close to real game conditions as you can get. It requires the defensive players to work together and the offensive players to work together.
- **Drill 12.5: Throw and Move.** This drill pits one player against another. Each player can switch from offense to defense. This is also a good aggression development drill.
- **Drill 12.6: Throw and Turn.** This drill teaches the defense how to move to the ball and turn the ball. It teaches the offense how to capture the ball before the defense can turn the ball.
- **Drill 12.8: Through the Box.** This drill requires a player to go through several levels of defense before shooting on goal.
- **Drill 12.13: Pass and Shoot.** This drill allows your players to make decisions on the field that result in passing the ball down the field and creating a shooting opportunity.
- **Drill 12.14: Chip and Shoot.** This drill is applicable to all playing situations. It can be performed during play or in a dead ball situation. Your players must be able to use the chip to advance the ball and create shooting opportunities.
- **Drill 12.19: Marking a Player.** This drill teaches players how to be better on defense. They play man-to-man, or one-on-one, while on defense, staying with their players. When their team gets the ball, they break away and become the offense. When their team loses the ball, each player must quickly pick up the player he or she is marking.

Problem

The team can move the ball down the field but *cannot finish with scoring*.

Solution

This is probably the most common complaint from coaches. Many teams can control the ball and move it down the field with relative ease, but they cannot score when they get the ball in the opposing team's goal area. In every case the problems and the solutions are the same.

The team generally lacks shooting confidence when they are in front of the goal. They feel confident when they are in control of the ball and are moving the ball down the field, but when faced with the defense, and the requirement to shoot, they shrink away from the act. Many players don't want to make mistakes in front of the goal. While moving the ball in the center of the field, they know it is okay if they make a mistake because they have room to regroup. They often only get one chance in front of the goal.

This problem is often a result of the coach telling players to wait until they have a good shot. The trouble with that advice is when players recognize that they are in position to take the good shot, it is often too late to take it. Compounding this problem is that many coaches don't want the players to be trigger-happy and shoot every time they get the ball.

As a coach you have to let the players know that the only mistake they can make in front of the goal is to not shoot. A bad shot is preferable to no shot at all. Tell them to trust their instincts. If they want to shoot, do it. When a player shoots the ball, congratulate that player, even if it was a bad shot. Accuracy will come from practice. All players want to be praised, and when they hear others being praised they too will get involved. Positive motivation goes a long way.

Another factor is that many players try to set up the ball for the perfect shot. As a result they lose the ball. There are very few times a player will get a perfect shot. They have to be taught in practice to shoot quickly and in different situations. The more different types of shooting drills you practice, the more confidence the players will have on the field.

Shooting Drills

- **Drills 10.1, 10.2, and 10.3: Shooting with Cone.** This is the first step to teach your players to shoot. These drills teach the proper way to kick the ball to have an effective shot.
- **Drill 10.4: Shooting with Both Feet.** This drill teaches players how to adjust to a ball coming to them from an angle and to shoot with one touch on the ball using both feet.

- **Drill 10.5: Catch the Ball and Shoot.** This drill teaches players to communicate, to quickly pick up the ball as it comes from behind, and to make a quick shot on goal.
- **Drill 10.6: Turn and Shoot.** This drill teaches players to shoot while moving across the face of the goal.
- **Drill 10.7: Redirect the Ball Shooting.** This drill teaches players how to properly redirect or deflect the ball. This is an effective method of scoring.

Many players will want to pass the ball to another player they think is better at shooting than them. As a result the ball is passed around until it is lost to the other team. Once the ball is passed into the open area of the goal, the next player who has the ball should shoot. Passing it too much will not put points on the board.

Combination Shooting Drills

- **Drill 11.9: Triangle Pass and Shoot.** This drill is a combination of passing the ball one direction and then having the ball returned in the opposite direction to the shooter, who is now in a better position to shoot on goal.
- **Drill 11.12: Flick and Move.** This drill teaches ball control, passing, and shooting on goal. It is not a move that is often used in play, but it does help develop touch on the ball and the ability to shoot on goal.

Offense and Defense Drills

- **Drill 12.1: Back and Forth to the Goal.** This drill is intended to place each player in a situation where he or she plays offense and defense.
- **Drill 12.2: Two on One.** This drill teaches players how to get the defense to commit, when to pass, and how to move to open space.
- **Drill 12.3: Two on Two.** This drill teaches players, offense and defense, to play as a team. It also requires the offensive players to move to keep the defense in a moving or chase position.
- **Drill 12.4: Three on Three.** This drill is as close to real game conditions as you can get. It requires the defensive players to work together and the offensive players to work together.

If your team is getting one shot and then loses the ball, it often means that your support players are not doing their jobs. When a player shoots, that player as well as other players must follow the ball. The ball can be dropped by the goalkeeper, deflect off of another player, or hit the post. There are many other things that could happen that would give your team another shot. Also, your halfbacks have to be ready for the ball to come back out of the goal area. If they are in proper position, they will be able to send the ball back in or restart the play by going to the outside and centering the ball.

Offense and Defense Drills

- **Drill 12.9: Center and Shoot.** This drill teaches your team how to center the ball in front of the goal to increase your scoring opportunities.
- **Drill 12.10: Corner Kick and Shoot.** This drill teaches your team how to properly execute a corner kick and how to defend against a corner kick. The principle of this drill is the same no matter how many players you use.
- **Drill 12.11: Throw-In and Shoot.** This drill teaches the throw-in. There are normally more throw-ins during a game than any other dead ball situation. Being able to gain an advantage is a must to win.
- **Drill 12.12: Goal Kick.** Goal kicks are similar to throw-ins in how often they occur during a game. Your team has to be able to clear the ball during a goal kick. Or, if the opposing team is kicking, your team must also be able to capture the ball.
- **Drill 12.13: Pass and Shoot.** This drill allows your players to make passing decisions on the field that result in moving the ball down the field and creating a shooting opportunity.

The final problem may be that the team is not bringing the ball down the field and centering it properly. When the offense brings the ball down the center, the defense has the ability to form and potentially keep the ball out of the goal area. When the ball is taken to the outside of the field and then centered, it causes the defense to be spread out, creating openings for the offense. Also, moving the ball keeps the defenders in motion and does not let them set up.

Combination Shooting Drills

- **Drill 11.10: Trail and Shoot.** This drill teaches players how to move the ball and to shadow the player with the ball to get a shooting opportunity.
- **Drill 11.11: Pass and Move.** This drill teaches passing, moving to open space, centering the ball, moving down the field, and shooting on goal. Essentially, this drill covers everything that is necessary to properly perform in a game.
- **Drill 11.13: Drop and Shoot.** A timing drill that uses passing, dribbling, and shooting, this drill teaches players to be aware of where they are on the field. It also requires communication with other players.

Offense and Defense Drills

- **Drill 12.4: Three on Three.** This drill is as close to real game conditions as you can get. It requires the defensive players to work together and the offensive players to work together.
- **Drill 12.9: Center and Shoot.** This drill teaches your team how to center the ball in front of the goal to increase your scoring opportunities.

Problem

My *fullbacks just kick the ball* rather than passing the ball or moving it up the field.

Solution

This is a natural action and is actually taught by many young coaches. The coaches do so as a method to get the ball out of the defense as fast as possible. The problem with this style of play is that players are just clearing the ball and not actually getting it to anyone in particular.

1. The players feel pressured and want to get rid of the ball. Many lack the skills to move the ball and pass to a teammate. Doing drills that will increase their skills will take the pressure off of them and give them confidence that they can make the moves without losing the ball. They will also find out that when they do lose the ball they can regain possession.
2. Many players will get into the habit of always doing the same thing. If the player is on the left side of the field, he or she might always move to the left, toward the touchline in order to kick with the left foot, or move away from the goal. All players must be able to move to the open space whether it is on the right or the left. When a player becomes predictable, the opposing players gain confidence and control of the situation.

Dribbling Drills

- **Drill 8.1: Basic Dribbling.** This drill teaches players the proper technique to use when dribbling.
- **Drill 8.2: Dribbling with Cone.** This drill teaches players to dribble with their heads up so they can see the field.
- **Drill 8.3: Reverse the Ball Dribble.** This drill helps players learn how to reverse the ball while dribbling.
- **Drill 8.4: Change Speed Dribbling.** This drill teaches players how to vary their speed while dribbling. This type of technique is a necessity for playing soccer.

Passing Drills

- **Drill 9.3: Pass to Moving Player Through Goal.** The point of this drill is for players to learn to pass with accuracy while moving, to communicate, and to provide support.
- **Drill 9.4: Rock 'Em Sock 'Em Passing.** This drill is great to teach players when to pass. Many players hold the ball too long or pass before it's appropriate. This drill teaches timing and the necessity for accuracy in the pass.
- **Drill 9.6: Pass Between Cones.** This drill teaches both the short pass and also passing and receiving with both feet.

Offense and Defense Drills

- **Drill 12.2: Two on One.** This drill teaches players how to get the defense to commit, when to pass, and how to move to open space.
- **Drill 12.3: Two on Two.** With this drill, players, offense and defense, learn to play as a team. It also requires the offensive players to move to keep the defense in a moving or chase position.
- **Drill 12.4: Three on Three.** This drill is as close to real game conditions as you can get. It requires the defensive players to work together and the offensive players to work together.
- **Drill 12.6: Throw and Turn.** This drill teaches the defense how to move to the ball and turn the ball. It teaches the offense how to capture the ball before the defense can turn it.
- **Drill 12.7: Chip and Turn.** This drill uses a chip to get the ball down the field. It is a one-on-one situation where the defense tries to get to the ball and turn it while the offense tries to capture the ball on the turn.
- **Drill 12.9: Center and Shoot.** Use this drill to teach your team how to center the ball. Getting the ball in front of the goal increases your scoring opportunities.
- **Drill 12.13: Pass and Shoot.** This drill allows your players to make decisions on the field that result in passing the ball down the field to create a shooting opportunity.
- **Drill 12.14: Chip and Shoot.** This drill is applicable to all playing situations. Ir can be performed during play or on a dead ball situation. Your players must be able to use the chip to advance the ball and create shooting opportunities.

Problem

My *team always loses the ball* as they try to move it from their defense to the other end of the field.

Solution

This is normally a lack of passing skills, but it can also be a lack of support for the player with the ball.

The first area to work on is passing skills. Many players do not know when to get rid of the ball and as a result hold it too long or pass too early. The player with the ball should hold the ball until challenged. When the opposing player has committed, that is the time to pass. The distance that the player can still pass safely is normally when the opposing player is two steps from the player with the ball.

The player with the ball has to have patience and, at the same time, know when to pass. Passing the ball before the player is actually challenged gives the opposing team the advantage to gain possession of the ball.

Passing Drills

- **Drill 9.3: Pass to Moving Player Through Goal.** The point of this drill is to teach players to pass with accuracy while moving, to communicate, and to provide support.
- **Drill 9.4: Rock 'Em Sock 'Em Passing.** This drill teaches players when to pass. Many players hold the ball too long or pass before it's appropriate. This drill teaches timing and passing accuracy.
- **Drill 9.6: Pass Between Cones.** This drill teaches both the short pass and passing and receiving with both feet.

Offense and Defense Drills

- **Drill 12.2: Two on One.** This drill teaches players how to get the defense to commit, when to pass, and how to move to open space.
- **Drill 12.3: Two on Two.** In this drill, players, offense and defense, play as a team. It also requires the offensive players to move to keep the defense in a moving or chase position.
- **Drill 12.4: Three on Three.** This drill is as close to real game conditions as you can get. It requires the defensive players to work together and the offensive players to work together.
- **Drill 12.13: Pass and Shoot.** This drill allows your players to make decisions on the field that result in passing the ball down the field and creating a shooting opportunity.
- **Drill 12.14: Chip and Shoot.** This drill is applicable to all playing situations and can be performed during play or on a dead ball situation. Your players must be able to use the chip to advance the ball and create shooting opportunities.

Many times when a player is moving the ball down the field and gets challenged, he or she doesn't have anyone to pass the ball to. Anytime you have a player moving with the ball, the players around this player must be moving to get into position to receive the ball. They cannot do this if they are on the back side of a player. They must move to open space.

This is formation play. Players must provide support from the front, back, and sides. The combination of proper passing and proper support will allow the team to move the ball down the field with efficiency.

Offense and Defense Drills

- **Drill 12.23: Zone Play.** This drill teaches players to stay in their areas of the field and to pass to other players.

Formations

- **Drill 15.1: Diamond/Triangle Position.** This formation provides balance and support.

Problem

How do I *teach my players to move the ball to the outside of the field* and keep it out of the center?

Solution

The first thing you need to convey to the team is how soccer formations are designed. Practically all soccer formations have the majority of players in the center of the field. Quite often half of the team will be in the center of the field. This leaves a quarter of the team on each side. Also, when the ball is in the center of the field, side players can easily converge into the center. When the ball is on the outside fewer players can actually converge to provide coverage. The players across the field cannot move to the far side without opening that side of the field. As a result, keeping the ball out of the center of the field and moving the ball to the side will give your team less opposition.

1. Passing, centering, and switching the ball drills are a plus to learning this style of play. Once players become comfortable with moving the ball down the side, they will continue. They will find out that they will lose the ball less on the outside than when they are trying to go straight down the center.

2. Moving the ball to the side causes the opposing team to shift their players, and when they are shifting to defend the ball, your team will be able to see openings to move the ball. Also, when the player takes the ball to the end line near the corner flag, that player has caused the defense to spread out, providing openings in front of the goal. All of this will encourage your players to continue moving the ball to the side.

Combination Shooting Drills
- **Drill 11.10: Trail and Shoot.** This drill teaches players how to move the ball and to shadow the player with the ball to get a shooting opportunity.
- **Drill 11.11: Pass and Move.** This drill teaches passing, moving to open space, centering the ball, moving down the field, and shooting on goal. It covers everything necessary to properly perform in a game.
- **Drill 11.13: Drop and Shoot.** This drill teaches players to be aware of where they are on the field and requires communication with other players. It is a timing drill that uses passing, dribbling, and shooting.

Offense and Defense Drills
- **Drill 12.4: Three on Three.** This drill is as close to real game conditions as you can get. It requires the defensive players to work together and the offensive players to work together.
- **Drill 12.13: Pass and Shoot.** This drill allows your players to make decisions on the field that result in passing the ball down the field to create a shooting opportunity.

Problem

My players *can't center the ball*.

Solution

All players can center the ball. It is just a matter of teaching the proper technique.

Start with centering, or getting the ball from the side of the field to the center of the field. Once you have the ball coming to the center of the field, then you can work on accuracy of both the centering kick and a shot on goal.

When you have distance and accuracy, then you can work on scoring off of the center. This is an area you should take in steps, and you will get the proper results.

Combination Shooting Drills

- **Drill 11.11: Pass and Move.** This drill teaches passing, moving to open space, centering the ball, moving down the field, and shooting on goal. It covers everything that is necessary to properly perform in a game.

Offense and Defense Drills

- **Drill 12.9: Center and Shoot.** This drill teaches your team how to center the ball in front of the goal to increase your scoring opportunities.
- **Drill 12.13: Pass and Shoot.** This drill allows your players to make decisions on the field that result in passing the ball down the field, creating a shooting opportunity.
- **Drill 12.14: Chip and Shoot.** Applicable to all playing situations, this drill can be performed during play or on a dead ball situation. Your players must be able to use the chip to advance the ball and create shooting opportunities.

Problem

My team *can't score off of dead ball situations*.

Solution

Many teams don't practice dead ball drills as much as they should. As a result the players don't know what to do when the situation arises. Not every player will be able to understand the techniques and, as a result, won't be able to accomplish a dead ball restart.

When practicing the drills, find your most effective players for each dead ball situation and always do it with the same players. The routine will become comfortable for all the players because they will know what is expected of them.

Throw-in drills can be incorporated with dribbling and shooting drills to teach your players how to take advantage of the situation.

Combination Shooting Drills

- **Drill 11.1: Head and Shoot.** In this individual drill, each player heads the ball and then moves to the ball and shoots on goal. This drill teaches heading, moving to the ball, and shooting on goal.
- **Drill 11.2: Head to Shooter.** This drill encourages heading, moving to the ball by another player, and shooting on goal.
- **Drill 11.3: Run to Goal Heading.** This drill develops the accuracy and strength necessary to direct the ball into the goal while on the move.

- **Drill 11.4: Side Heading.** The purpose of this drill is to head the ball into the goal while running straight on the ball, heading the ball to the left or right corners of the goal.
- **Drill 11.5: Throw and Shoot.** Throwing distance is as important as accuracy. This drill teaches players to throw the ball high and far.
- **Drill 11.6: Throw, Head, and Shoot.** The ability to throw, head, and shoot is very valuable. This drill lets the players get creative on all of the techniques.
- **Drill 11.7: Turn and Shoot.** This drill uses the throw-in, heading, and different techniques for receiving the ball. It also incorporates dribbling and shooting.
- **Drill 11.8: Throw-In and Shoot.** This drill trains players to gauge the proper placement for a throw-in. It trains both the player doing the throw-in and the player receiving the ball.

Offense and Defense Drills

- **Drill 12.5: Throw and Move.** This drill pits one player against another and requires the player to start by winning the ball. Each player can switch from offense to defense. This is also a good aggression development drill.
- **Drill 12.6: Throw and Turn.** This drill teaches the defense how to move to and turn the ball. It teaches the offense how to capture the ball before the defense can turn it.
- **Drill 12.11: Throw-In and Shoot.** This drill teaches the throw-in. There are normally more throw-ins during a game than any other dead ball situation. Being able to gain an advantage is a must to win.

Direct and indirect penalty plays should be a normal part of position play during your practices. This will teach players what to do and how to properly execute the play. Since you are doing it during position play, you may have to call the ball back and repeat the situation until all players are reacting properly.

Offense and Defense Drills

- **Drills 12.20 and 12.21: Indirect Kick.** These drills teach your team to properly execute an indirect penalty kick. Using proper technique improves your team's ability to score.
- **Drill 12.22: Direct Kick.** This drill teaches your team how to properly execute a direct penalty kick. Using proper technique results in a great opportunity to score.

A kickoff should not be just kicking the ball down the field. When doing a kickoff the ball should be placed to another player so that your team maintains control of the ball. This can also be taught during position play.

Offense and Defense Drills

- **Drill 12.9: Center and Shoot.** Use this drill to teach your team how to center the ball. Getting the ball in front of the goal increases your scoring opportunities.

Corner kicks, penalty kicks, and goal kicks all have designated ways to be done. This is another area that should be incorporated into position play. You can also teach these as part of the cooldown drills. Doing them more often allows your players to improve performance and skill. Work these skills into position play and cooldown for maximum effectiveness.

Offense and Defense Drills

- **Drill 12.10: Corner Kick and Shoot.** This drill teaches your team how to properly execute a corner kick and how to defend against it. The principle of this drill is the same no matter how many players you use.
- **Drill 12.12: Goal Kick.** Goal kicks are right up there with throw-ins as to the number performed during a game. Your team has to be able to clear the ball during a goal kick. Your team must also be able to capture the ball if the opposing team is kicking.
- **Drill 12.15: Goal Kick and Return.** This drill is used to teach players how to receive a hard-kicked ball and then how to quickly shoot on goal.
- **Drill 12.16: Corner Kick Accuracy and Shoot.** This drill improves the accuracy of the corner kick and also allows your players to be able to move to adjust on the ball coming from the kick.
- **Drill 12.18: Dribble, Clear, and Shoot.** A great way to improve offensive moves, this drill is a one-on-one with the goalkeeper. The player must get past the goalkeeper before shooting on goal.

Problem

I *can't get my players to shoot* when they are open.

Solution

This is similar to the problem of a team not being able to finish. As stated earlier, the players need two things—confidence and improved shooting skills.

Confidence usually improves with the skill, but you must let players know you want them to shoot, even if they miss or don't score. Players can't score if they don't shoot.

The most common reason for players not shooting is that they lack confidence when in front of the goal. Players often feel confident when moving the ball down the field, but when faced with the defense and the requirement to shoot they shrink away from doing so. Many players don't want to make mistakes in front of the goal. When moving the ball down the center of the field, they know it is okay if they make a mistake because they have room to regroup. But they only get one chance in front of the goal.

As mentioned previously, this is often a result of the coach telling players to wait until they have a good shot. The problem is that by the time they recognize they have a good shot, it is often too late to take it. Also, many coaches don't want players to be trigger-happy and shoot every time they get the ball.

As a coach you have to let your players know that the only mistake they can make in front of the goal is to not shoot. A bad shot is preferable to no shot. Tell them to trust their instincts. If they want to shoot, do it. When you get a player to shoot on goal, compliment them, even if the shot was bad. Accuracy comes from working on specific shooting drills. Players like to be praised, and when they are, they will do more to get more praise. The other players will hear this, and they will shoot so they can be praised, too.

Once you have them shooting, it is just a matter of improving their skills to the point where they can place the ball into the net, away from the goalkeeper.

Shooting Drills

- **Drills 10.1, 10.2, and 10.3: Shooting with Cone.** This is the first step to teach your players to shoot. Use these drills to teach the proper way to kick the ball to have an effective shot.

Combination Shooting Drills

- **Drill 11.11: Pass and Move.** This drill teaches passing, moving to open space, centering the ball, moving down the field, and shooting on goal. This drill covers everything that is necessary to properly perform in a game.
- **Drill 11.12: Flick and Move.** This drill teaches ball control, passing, and shooting on goal. It is not an on-field move that is often used, but it is helpful to develop touch on the ball and the ability to shoot on goal.

Offense and Defense Drills

- **Drill 12.1: Back and Forth to the Goal.** This drill places each player in a situation to play offense and defense.
- **Drill 12.2: Two on One.** This drill teaches players how to get the defense to commit, when to pass, and how to move to open space.

Another factor in not shooting is that many players try to set up the ball for the perfect shot. As a result they lose the ball to the defense. There are very few times a player will get a perfect shot. They have to be taught in practice to shoot quickly and in different situations. Shooting fast without settling the ball gives the shooter an advantage. The more types of shooting drills you practice, the more confidence the players will have on the field.

Shooting Drills

- **Drill 10.4: Shooting with Both Feet.** This drill teaches players how to adjust to a ball coming to them from an angle and to shoot with one touch on the ball using either foot.
- **Drill 10.5: Catch the Ball and Shoot.** This drill encourages players to communicate, to quickly pick up the ball as it comes from behind, and to take a quick shot on goal.
- **Drill 10.6: Turn and Shoot.** This drill teaches players to shoot while moving across the face of the goal.
- **Drill 10.7: Redirect the Ball Shooting.** This drill teaches players how to properly redirect or deflect the ball. This is an effective method of scoring.

Combination Shooting Drills

- **Drill 11.13: Drop and Shoot.** This drill teaches players to be aware of where they are on the field. It also requires communication with other players. It is a timing drill that uses passing, dribbling, and shooting.
- **Drill 11.14: Self Half Volley Shot.** This drill helps players learn to shoot while the ball is in the air but on a bounce.
- **Drill 11.15: Throw Half Volley Shot.** This drill helps players move to the ball and shoot while the ball is in the air but on a bounce.
- **Drill 11.16: Self Full Volley Shot.** This drill allows players to move to the ball and shoot while the ball is still in the air and has not touched the ground.
- **Drill 11.17: Throw Full Volley Shot.** This drill allows the players to be able to move to the ball and shoot while the ball is in the air and has not touched the ground.

Offense and Defense Drills

- **Drill 12.3: Two on Two.** This drill teaches players, offense and defense, to play as a team. It also requires the offensive players to move to keep the defense in a moving or chase position.
- **Drill 12.4: Three on Three.** This drill is as close to real game conditions as you can get. It requires the defensive players to work together and the offensive players to work together.

Many players will want to pass the ball to another player they think is better at shooting than they are. As a result the ball is often passed around until it is lost to the other team. Once the ball is passed into the face area of the goal, the next player that has the ball should shoot. Press your players to try. Once they score, they will continue to shoot because now they know they can. Passing it too much will not put points on the board.

Combination Shooting Drills

- **Drill 11.9: Triangle Pass and Shoot.** This drill is a combination of passing the ball one direction and then having the ball returned in the opposite direction to the shooter, who is now in a better position to shoot on goal.
- **Drill 11.10: Trail and Shoot.** This drill teaches players how to move the ball and to shadow the player with the ball to get a shooting opportunity.

Offense and Defense Drills

- **Drill 12.5: Throw and Move.** This drill pits one player against another and requires the player to start by winning the ball. Each player can switch from offense to defense. This is also a good aggression development drill.
- **Drill 12.8: Through the Box.** This drill requires a player to go through several levels of defense before shooting on goal.

If your team is getting one shot and then losing the ball, it is often because your support players are not doing their jobs. When a player shoots, that player as well as the other players around the shooter must follow the ball. The ball can be dropped by the goalkeeper, can be deflected off of another player, or can hit the post. There are many things that can happen that will give your team another shot.

In addition, your halfbacks have to be ready for the ball to come back out of the goal area. If they are in proper position, they will be able to send the ball back in or restart the play by going to the outside and centering the ball.

Offense and Defense Drills

- **Drill 12.9: Center and Shoot.** With this drill, your team learns how to center the ball to get the ball in front of the goal, increasing scoring opportunities.
- **Drill 12.10: Corner Kick and Shoot.** This drill teaches your team how to properly execute a corner kick and how to defend against one. The principle of this drill is the same no matter how many players you use.
- **Drill 12.11: Throw-In and Shoot.** This drill teaches the throw-in. There are normally more throw-ins during a game than any other dead ball situation. Being able to gain an advantage with this skill is a must to win games.
- **Drill 12.12: Goal Kick.** Goal kicks are comparable with throw-ins in the number performed during a game. Your team has to be able to clear the ball during a goal kick. Or, if the opposing team is kicking, your team must be able to capture the ball.
- **Drill 12.13: Pass and Shoot.** This drill allows your players to make decisions during play that result in passing the ball down the field and creating a shooting opportunity.

Formations

- **Drill 15.2: Position Play.** This drill uses a controlled scrimmage to improve players' skills.

Problem

My players *can't get the ball past* the other team's defense.

Solution

This is caused by a lack of ball control skills. It may be in the form of passing, dribbling, or control of the ball.

Drills that place players into situations where they are required to be one-on-one with other players will improve their dribbling and ball control skills.

Passing drills improve the ability to move the ball when trapped or to create movement of the ball.

Dribbling Drills

- **Drill 8.1: Basic Dribbling.** Use this drill to teach players proper dribbling technique.
- **Drill 8.2: Dribbling with Cone.** This drill teaches players to dribble with their heads up so they can see the field.

- **Drill 8.3: Reverse the Ball Dribble.** With this drill, players learn how to reverse the ball while dribbling.
- **Drill 8.4: Change Speed Dribbling.** This drill teaches players how to vary their speed while dribbling, an essential skill for playing soccer.
- **Drill 8.5: Step Over Right/Left Dribbling.** This drill helps players learn how to move the ball left and right while faking out the defense.
- **Drill 8.6: Fake Kick Dribbling.** This is a fake kick done while dribbling. This move often freezes the defender, allowing the player with the ball to move around that defending player.
- **Drill 8.7: Turn and Dribble.** This drill teaches players how to reverse a ball that is coming straight at them from the front.

Passing Drills

- **Drill 9.3: Pass to Moving Player Through Goal.** This drill promotes passing with accuracy while moving, communication among players, and providing support.
- **Drill 9.4: Rock 'Em Sock 'Em Passing.** This drill is great to teach players when to pass. Many players hold the ball too long or pass before it's appropriate. This drill teaches timing and the necessity for accuracy in the pass.
- **Drill 9.5: Wall Pass.** The wall pass is a very effective method for moving around an opponent while maintaining control of the ball. This drill teaches the basics of working with a teammate to move past an opponent.
- **Drill 9.6: Pass Between Cones.** With this drill, players learn the short pass and also how to pass and receive with both feet.

Placing the players in a two-on-one situation will require them to dribble, control the ball, and pass.

Offense and Defense Drills

- **Drill 12.9: Center and Shoot.** This drill teaches your team how to center the ball to get it in front of the goal, increasing your scoring opportunities.
- **Drill 12.13: Pass and Shoot.** This drill allows your players to make decisions during play that result in passing the ball down the field and creating a shooting opportunity.
- **Drill 12.14: Chip and Shoot.** Applicable to all playing situations, this drill can be performed during play or on a dead ball situation. Your players must be able to use the chip to advance the ball and create shooting opportunities.

Problem

I *can't get my players to hold their positions*; they move all over the field.

Solution

When players start in the game they normally play what is called "bunch play." The whole team bunches together, and everyone moves to the ball. You do not want to discourage this in younger players who are just beginning. They are learning to go to the ball, and that is exactly what you want.

As players learn to pass, this normally opens the field, although you may still have players grouping together. Be patient. You won't be able to tie boards to the players to keep them separated. What you can do is teach the technique called support.

Support is when the player with the ball has multiple outlets to get rid of the ball. There should always be a player in front, behind, and at the side or sides of the player with the ball. Teaching support promotes separation, and players learn to hold their positions.

Offense and Defense Drills

- **Drill 12.9: Center and Shoot.** This drill teaches your team how to center the ball to get it in front of the goal, increasing your scoring opportunities.
- **Drill 12.10: Corner Kick and Shoot.** This drill teaches your team how to properly execute a corner kick and how to defend against it. The principle of this drill is the same no matter how many players you use.
- **Drill 12.11: Throw-In and Shoot.** Use this drill to teach the throw-in. There are normally more throw-ins during a game than any other dead ball situation. Being able to gain an advantage with this skill is a must to win.
- **Drill 12.12: Goal Kick.** Goal kicks are comparable with throw-ins in the number performed during a game. Your team has to be able to clear the ball during a goal kick. Or, if the opposing team is kicking, your team must also be able to capture the ball.
- **Drill 12.14: Chip and Shoot.** This drill applies to all playing situations. The skill can be performed during play or on a dead ball situation. Your players must be able to use the chip to advance the ball and create shooting opportunities.
- **Drill 12.23: Zone Play.** This drill teaches players to stay in their areas of the field and to pass to other players.

Formations

- **Drill 15.1: Diamond/Triangle Position.** This formation fosters team balance and support.

It is a natural instinct to want to be involved in the play and have the ball. That is why you often see players move and take the ball away from their own teammates. Once you have taught support, and the players are maintaining this support, it is time to put them in position play. As players practice, stop play when players move out of position. Move them back into position and then resume play. Players will eventually understand where they need to be and, with continued practice and reinforcement, will stay in their positions.

Offense and Defense Drills

- **Drill 12.2: Two on One.** This drill teaches players how to get the defense to commit, when to pass, and how to move to open space.
- **Drill 12.3: Two on Two.** With this drill, players, offense and defense, learn to play as a team. It also requires the offensive players to move to keep the defense in a moving or chase position.
- **Drill 12.4: Three on Three.** This drill is as close to real game conditions as you can get. It requires the defensive players to work together and the offensive players to work together.
- **Drill 12.13: Pass and Shoot.** This drill allows your players to make decisions on the field that result in passing the ball down the field, creating a shooting opportunity.
- **Drill 12.19: Marking a Player.** This drill teaches players how to be better on defense. They play man-to-man, or one-on-one, while on defense, staying with their player. When their team gets the ball, they break away and become the offense. When their team loses the ball, they must quickly pick up the players they are marking.

Formations

- **Drill 15.2: Position Play.** This drill teaches through a controlled scrimmage.

Problem

My team *can't move the ball from the fullbacks to the forwards.*

Solution

This is normally because the halfbacks either are out of position or not maintaining control of the midfield. As a result, the ball will travel from the forwards to the fullbacks or directly from the fullbacks to the forwards. If the opposing team has halfbacks who are maintaining their positions, the ball is intercepted in midfield, keeping the ball from reaching your forwards.

Position play is a must to ensure your team works as one. The fullbacks must be able to move to open areas to pass. Your halfbacks need to move in unison with the fullbacks so they too can get open to receive the ball. The forwards must do the same thing. Only when players act together as a team will you solve this problem.

Offense and Defense Drills

- **Drill 12.1: Back and Forth to the Goal.** This drill is intended to place each player in a situation where he or she plays offense and defense.
- **Drill 12.2: Two on One.** Using this drill teaches players how to get the defense to commit, when to pass, and how to move to open space.
- **Drill 12.3: Two on Two.** This drill teaches players, offense and defense, to play as a team. It also requires the offensive players to move to keep the defense in a moving or chase position.
- **Drill 12.4: Three on Three.** This drill is as close to real game conditions as you can get. It requires the defensive players to work together and the offensive players to work together.
- **Drill 12.9: Center and Shoot.** Use this drill to teach your team how to center the ball. Getting the ball in front of the goal increases your scoring opportunities.
- **Drill 12.13: Pass and Shoot.** This drill allows your players to make decisions on the field that result in passing the ball down the field, creating a shooting opportunity.
- **Drill 12.14: Chip and Shoot.** This drill applies to all playing situations, and the skill can be performed during play or on a dead ball situation. Your players must be able to use the chip to advance the ball and create shooting opportunities.
- **Drill 12.23: Zone Play.** This drill teaches players to stay in their areas of the field and to pass to other players.

Another reason fullbacks may not be able to move the ball to the forwards is your players' lack of skill in passing and receiving the ball. The passes must be sharp, accurate, and without delay. Players must also have support.

Offense and Defense Drills

- **Drill 12.1: Back and Forth to the Goal.** This drill places each player in a situation to play offense and defense.
- **Drill 12.2: Two on One.** With this drill players learn how to get the defense to commit, when to pass, and how to move to open space.
- **Drill 12.3: Two on Two.** This drill teaches players, offense and defense, to play as a team. It also requires the offensive players to move to keep the defense in a moving or chase position.
- **Drill 12.4: Three on Three.** This drill is as close to real game conditions as you can get. It requires the defensive players to work together and the offensive players to work together.
- **Drill 12.5: Throw and Move.** This is a good aggression development drill that pits one player against another. Each player can switch from offense to defense, and it requires the player to start by winning the ball.
- **Drill 12.6: Throw and Turn.** This drill teaches the defense how to move to and turn the ball. It teaches the offense how to capture the ball before the defense can turn the ball.
- **Drill 12.7: Chip and Turn.** This drill uses a chip to get the ball down the field. It creates a one-on-one situation in which the defense tries to get to the ball and turn it as the offense tries to capture the ball on the turn.
- **Drill 12.8: Through the Box.** This drill requires a player to go through several levels of defense before shooting on goal.
- **Drill 12.15: Goal Kick and Return.** This drill teaches players how to receive a hard-kicked ball and quickly shoot on the goal.
- **Drill 12.16: Corner Kick Accuracy and Shoot.** Use this drill to improve the accuracy of the corner kick. It also helps your players learn to adjust on the ball coming from the kick.
- **Drill 12.17: Chip or Shoot.** This shooting-on-goal drill gives each player the opportunity to learn when he or she should chip or shoot directly on goal.
- **Drill 12.18: Dribble, Clear, and Shoot.** This drill is a one-on-one with the goalkeeper. The player must get past the goalkeeper before shooting on goal. This is great to improve offensive moves.
- **Drill 12.19: Marking a Player.** Use this drill to help players improve their defense. They play man-to-man, or one-on-one, while on defense, staying with their players. When their team gets the ball, they break away and become the offense. When their team loses the ball, they must quickly pick up the players they are marking.

Problem

My *players are always getting faked out* by the other players' moves.

Solution

Many times the players are watching the other players rather than the ball.

Players can fake right or left, move their feet quickly, and do a multitude of other moves, but the ball can only go where it is moved. Your players must watch the ball. Watching the movement of the ball is also a must in order for players to know when to move to intercept the ball.

Dribbling Drills

- **Drill 8.5: Step Over Right/Left Dribbling.** This drill teaches players how to move the ball left and right while faking out the defense.
- **Drill 8.6: Fake Kick Dribbling.** This is a fake kick done while dribbling. This skill often freezes the defender, allowing the player with the ball to move around that defending player.
- **Drill 8.7: Turn and Dribble.** This drill teaches players to reverse a ball coming straight to them from the front.

Passing Drills

- **Drill 9.4: Rock 'Em Sock 'Em Passing.** This drill is great for teaching players when to pass. Many players hold the ball too long or pass before it's appropriate. This drill teaches timing and the necessity for passing accuracy.

The core of individual defense is the ability to strip the ball from the opponent. One-on-one drills will improve players' individual abilities and timing.

Offense and Defense Drills

- **Drill 12.1: Back and Forth to the Goal.** With this drill each player plays offense and defense.
- **Drill 12.5: Throw and Move.** This drill pits one player against another. Each player can switch from offense to defense, and it requires the player to start by winning the ball. This is also a good aggression development drill.
- **Drill 12.6: Throw and Turn.** This drill teaches the defense how to move to and turn the ball. It teaches the offense how to capture the ball before the defense can turn it.

- **Drill 12.7: Chip and Turn.** This drill uses a chip to get the ball down the field. It creates a one-on-one situation in which the defense tries to get to the ball and turn it as the offense tries to capture the ball on the turn.
- **Drill 12.8: Through the Box.** In this drill a player goes through several levels of defense before he or she can shoot on goal.

Problem

My players are *unable to turn the ball* without losing the ball.

Solution

Most times this happens because a player has not gained control of the ball and tries to make a move before getting control. Quite often it is a result of not knowing the different ways to turn the ball.

When a closely covered player receives the ball and stops it, he or she has numerous options to turn the ball. The player can also dribble to open space.

Dribbling Drills

- **Drill 8.3: Reverse the Ball Dribble.** With this drill players learn how to reverse the ball while dribbling.
- **Drill 8.4: Change Speed Dribbling.** This drill teaches players how to vary their speed while dribbling, a necessity for playing soccer.
- **Drill 8.5: Step Over Right/Left Dribbling.** This drill teaches players how to move the ball left and right while faking out the defense.
- **Drill 8.6: Fake Kick Dribbling.** This is a fake kick done while dribbling. This skill often freezes the defender, allowing the player with the ball to move around that defending player.

Offense and Defense Drills

- **Drill 12.1: Back and Forth to the Goal.** This drill places each player in a situation where he or she plays offense and defense.
- **Drill 12.5: Throw and Move.** A good aggression development drill, this drill pits one player against another. Each player can switch from offense to defense.

When the player isn't closely covered, there are different options to turn the ball and move quickly down the field. This can be through learned techniques or simply by the player letting the ball roll past and moving to the ball.

Dribbling Drills

- **Drill 8.7: Turn and Dribble.** This drill teaches players to reverse a ball that is coming straight at them from the front.

Offense and Defense Drills

- **Drill 12.6: Throw and Turn.** This drill teaches the defense how to move to the ball and turn the ball. It teaches the offense how to capture the ball before the defense can turn it.
- **Drill 12.7: Chip and Turn.** This drill uses a chip to get the ball down the field. It is a one-on-one situation where the defense tries to get to the ball and turn it while the offense tries to capture the ball on the turn.

Problem

My team *can't stop opposing goals* from being scored by crosses or corner kicks.

Solution

This is another area where there can be multiple problems, yet all of them directly relate to position play.

The fullbacks are not moving properly and, as a result, end up with a two-on-one situation.

Offense and Defense Drills

- **Drill 12.9: Center and Shoot.** Use this drill to teach your team how to center the ball. Getting the ball in front of the goal increases your scoring opportunities. It also teaches your team how to defend against a center. You can improve your offense and at the same time work with your defense to counter the play.
- **Drill 12.10: Corner Kick and Shoot.** This drill teaches your team how to properly execute a corner kick and how to defend against one. The principle of this drill is the same no matter how many players you use.

    The fullback does not mark the player with the ball, allowing that player to get off a center kick without any pressure.

Offense and Defense Drills

- **Drill 12.1: Back and Forth to the Goal.** This drill places each player in a situation to play offense and defense.

- **Drill 12.5: Throw and Move.** This drill pits one player against another, and it requires the player to start by winning the ball. Each player can switch from offense to defense This is also a good aggression development drill.
- **Drill 12.6: Throw and Turn.** This drill teaches the defense how to move to the ball and turn it. It teaches the offense how to capture the ball before the defense can turn it.
- **Drill 12.7: Chip and Turn.** This drill uses a chip to get the ball down the field. It creates a one-on-one situation where the defense tries to get to the ball and turn it as the offense tries to capture the ball on the turn.
- **Drill 12.8: Through the Box.** In this drill a player goes through several levels of defense before he or she can shoot on goal.
- **Drill 12.18: Dribble, Clear, and Shoot.** This drill is a one-on-one with the goalkeeper. The player must get past the goalkeeper before shooting on goal. This is a great drill to improve offensive moves.
- **Drill 12.19: Marking a Player.** Use this drill to help players improve their defense. They play man-to-man, or one-on-one, while on defense, staying with their players. When their team gets the ball, they break away and become the offense. When their team loses the ball, they must quickly pick up the players they are marking.

  The fullbacks do not position themselves in front of the goal so they can cover all of the opposing players.

Offense and Defense Drills

- **Drill 12.10: Corner Kick and Shoot.** This drill teaches your team how to properly execute a corner kick and how to defend against one. The principle of this drill is the same no matter how many players you use.
- **Drill 12.13: Pass and Shoot.** With this drill, your players learn to make decisions on the field that result in moving the ball down the field and creating a shooting opportunity.
- **Drill 12.14: Chip and Shoot.** This drill applies to all playing situations, and the skill can be performed during play or on a dead ball situation. Your players must be able to use the chip to advance the ball and create shooting opportunities.
- **Drill 12.23: Zone Play.** This drill teaches players to stay in their areas of the field and to pass to other players.

  The goalkeeper does not come out of the goal to catch or cut off the cross of the ball.

Offense and Defense Drills

- **Drill 12.12: Goal Kick.** Goal kicks are comparable to throw-ins as to the number performed during a game. Your team has to be able to clear the ball during a goal kick. Or, if the opposing team is kicking, your team must also be able to capture the ball.
- **Drill 12.15: Goal Kick and Return.** Use this drill to teach players how to receive a hard-kicked ball and then quickly shoot on goal.
- **Drill 12.17: Chip or Shoot.** This drill is a shooting on goal drill. It gives each player the opportunity to learn when he or she should chip or shoot directly on goal.

Goalkeeper Drills

- **Drill 13.1: Ground Catch.** This drill teaches the goalkeeper how to catch and scoop the ball when it is coming on the ground.
- **Drill 13.2: Hand Positions for Catching Ball.** With this drill, the goalkeeper learns proper hand positions. This is one of numerous techniques the goalkeeper must know to properly handle and control the ball.
- **Drill 13.3: In the Air Catch.** This drill teaches the goalkeeper how to catch and control the ball when it is coming through the air.

When the goalkeeper stays inside the goal, the areas to his or her right and left are open and the opponent has the advantage. The opponent can shoot, knowing the goalkeeper cannot get to the ball. By moving out of the goal, the goalkeeper gains the advantage by decreasing the open space in the goal. Teach your goalkeepers to move, not stand in the goal. The following drills illustrate how movement decreases open areas.

- **Drills 13.4, 13.5, and 13.6: Movement to the Ball.** Movement in the goal area is essential. These drills teach the goalkeeper the proper position in relation to the goal and the player with the ball. The goalkeeper must constantly move to decrease the shooting advantage.
- **Drill 13.7: Kick and Return.** This drill teaches the goalkeeper to move throughout the penalty area to gain possession of the ball. It also works on the goalkeeper's kick or throw.
- **Drill 13.8: Corner Kick.** With this drill the goalkeeper learns how to move for the ball during a corner kick. He or she can catch the ball or punch the ball to clear it from the goal area.
- **Drill 13.9: Penalty Kick.** This drill teaches the goalkeeper how to respond to a penalty kick.

- **Drill 13.10: Throw and Return.** Use this drill to teach the goalkeeper to throw the ball with accuracy. It also allows the goalkeeper to play a shot on goal.

Problem

My *team is unable to pass,* or their passes are intercepted by the other team.

Solution

This is usually the result of holding the ball too long or passing the ball before the opponent has committed.

If the player passing the ball is not using proper passing techniques, his or her passes will not have the strength or accuracy necessary to reach the other players. Many times this is because the player is dribbling with the head down and is not able to see players who are open.

Dribbling Drills
- **Drill 8.2: Dribbling with Cone.** This drill helps players learn how to dribble with their heads up so they can see the field.

Not knowing when to pass can result in the player holding the ball too long and losing the ball. Passing too early allows the opposing players to play the player receiving the ball rather than having to play the player with the ball. If you don't pull the opposing players to the ball, you will have no one to pass to.

Passing Drills
- **Drill 9.4: Rock 'Em Sock 'Em Passing.** This drill is great to teach players when to pass. Many players hold the ball too long or pass before it's appropriate. This drill teaches them timing and accurate passes.
- **Drill 9.6: Pass Between Cones.** This drill improves the short pass and also passing and receiving with either foot.
- **Drill 9.10: Pass Through Legs.** The ability to pass to the feet of another player is a must in soccer. This drill teaches players the proper place to pass and how to receive by going to the ball.

Problem

My team is *unable to stop or intercept the passes* from the other team.

Solution

This is not as big a problem as it seems. Most likely your players do not understand the concept of coverage. There are simple steps that explain the principles of defense. These principles use basic concepts that let you provide proper defensive coverage.

When the opposing team gains control of the ball, the nearest player becomes the first defender. That player sticks with the player with the ball to try and gain possession of the ball. This enables teammates to regroup and cover the other players.

Offense and Defense Drills

- **Drill 12.1: Back and Forth to the Goal.** This drill places each player in a situation where he or she plays offense and defense.
- **Drill 12.2: Two on One.** This drill teaches players how to get the defense to commit, when to pass, and how to move to open space.
- **Drill 12.5: Throw and Move.** In this aggression development drill, players are pitted against each other. Play begins when a player wins the ball, and each player can switch from offense to defense.
- **Drill 12.13: Pass and Shoot.** This drill allows your players to make decisions on the field that result in passing the ball down the field, creating a shooting opportunity.
- **Drill 12.23: Zone Play.** This drill teaches players to stay in their areas of the field and to pass to other players.

Your players must be in position to cut off the pass or intercept it. They cannot stay behind the opposing players and always allow them to gain control of the ball.

Offense and Defense Drills

- **Drill 12.3: Two on Two.** This drill teaches players, offense and defense, to play as a team. It also requires the offensive players to move to keep the defense in a moving or chase position.
- **Drill 12.4: Three on Three.** This drill is as close to real game conditions as you can get. It requires the defensive players to work together and the offensive players to work together.

- **Drill 12.9: Center and Shoot.** Use this drill to teach your team how to center the ball. Getting the ball in front of the goal increases your scoring opportunities.
- **Drill 12.13: Pass and Shoot.** This drill allows your players to make decisions on the field that result in passing the ball down the field, creating a shooting opportunity.
- **Drill 12.14: Chip and Shoot.** This drill applies to all playing situations. Chipping can be performed during play or on a dead ball situation. Your players must be able to use the chip to advance the ball and create shooting opportunities.

Problem

My team always *loses in the last 10 to 15 minutes* of the game.

Solution

This is almost always caused by lack of proper conditioning. It can also be caused by poor organization, which will get worse as the game progresses.

If your team is not properly conditioned, they will experience fatigue near the end of the game. Drills that encourage cardiovascular endurance are a must.

Conditioning Drills

- **Drill 14.1: Pass and Run.** This simple conditioning drill requires players to move with the ball. They dribble, pass, and run.
- **Drill 14.2: Move with or Without Ball.** This drill is a good cardiovascular drill to build stamina. It requires a mixture of short jogs and runs and can be done with or without the ball. If done with the ball, it teaches your players how to move fast and then slow while maintaining control of the ball.
- **Drill 14.3: Run Then Jog.** This conditioning drill requires players to move around cones rather than go in a straight line. It can be done with or without the ball.
- **Drill 14.4: Beat the Ball.** Use this drill for conditioning and improving speed dribbling.
- **Drill 14.5: Move to the Front.** This is a formation drill that requires players to sprint to the front of the line.
- **Drill 14.6: Cross Field Jog/Run.** Jogging and running are alternated in this conditioning drill. Dribbling can be included if you want your players to have more time on the ball.

- **Drill 14.7: Station Run.** This drill, which does not use a ball, builds cardiovascular endurance.
- **Drill 14.8: Jump Cones.** This is a conditioning drill that helps develop the lateral jump.
- **Drill 14.9: Front/Back Race.** With this drill, players improve their conditioning and learn to move backward with balance.
- **Drill 14.10: Touch Cone.** This is a running drill that requires the player to bend down and touch the cone while on a full run.

Not using your substitutes properly will cause players on the field to go beyond their conditioning level while others are fresh and ready to play. You must have players who you can substitute into all areas of play.

Lack of organization and training can result in the team losing confidence, especially if the other team is ahead at the time. Proper training with drills, organized practices, and proper discipline is a must.

Problem

My team is *unable to stop the other team from scoring* off of fast breaks.

Solution

You have a fullback problem as well as a goalkeeper problem.

Many teams put their bigger, slower players in the defense. They think that this is the best place for them. It is not. You must have fullbacks that are as skilled and as fast as the remainder of the team. They must also know the proper defensive actions to stop or put pressure on a player on a fast break.

Offense and Defense Drills

- **Drill 12.1: Back and Forth to the Goal.** This drill places each player in a situation to play offense and defense.
- **Drill 12.5: Throw and Move.** This drill pits one player against another. Each player can switch from offense to defense. This is also a good aggression development drill.

Many times when a player is on a fast break, the goalkeeper doesn't come out of the goal to challenge that player. This gives the player with the ball the advantage.

Goalkeeper Drills

- **Drills 13.4, 13.5, and 13.6: Movement to the Ball.** Movement in the goal area is essential. These drills teach the goalkeeper the proper position in relation to the goal and the player with the ball. The goalkeeper must constantly move to decrease the shooting advantage.
- **Drill 13.7: Kick and Return.** This drill teaches the goalkeeper to move throughout the penalty area to gain possession of the ball. It also works on the goalkeeper's kick or throw.
- **Drill 13.10: Throw and Return.** This drill teaches the goalkeeper to throw the ball with accuracy. It also allows the goalkeeper to play a shot on goal.

Problem

The opposing team *scores too much off our goal kicks*.

Solution

Many times this is a result of using the wrong player to take the goal kick or kicking the ball to the wrong place. Your field players must cover the opposing team and provide an outlet for the player kicking the goal kick.

1. If you do not have players who can kick the ball over the heads of the players on the penalty box line, then have them kick the ball to the side so the ball cannot be returned directly back into the goal.
2. Keep your goalkeeper in the goal rather than letting him or her take the kick.
3. Keep defensive players inside the penalty area rather than sending all of them out of the goal area.
4. Make sure all opposing players around the penalty box area are covered.

Offense and Defense Drills

- **Drill 12.12: Goal Kick.** Goal kicks are similar to throw-ins in the number performed during a game. Your team has to be able to clear the ball during a goal kick. Or, if the opposing team is kicking, your team must also be able to capture the ball.
- **Drill 12.15: Goal Kick and Return.** This drill teaches players how to receive a hard-kicked ball and then quickly shoot on goal.
- **Drill 12.18: Dribble, Clear, and Shoot.** This drill is a one-on-one with the goalkeeper. The player must get past the goalkeeper before shooting on goal. This is a great drill to improve offensive moves.

Goalkeeper Drills
- **Drill 13.10: Throw and Return.** This drill teaches the goalkeeper to throw the ball with accuracy. It also allows the goalkeeper to play a shot on goal.

Problem

After our team shoots on the other team's goal, the *opposing team quickly moves the ball* to our end of the field *and scores*.

Solution

This is the result of two main issues. When all of your players move into the goal area, there is no one left in midfield to capture the ball when it comes out. As a result the ball moves right to your fullbacks or, in many cases, right past your fullbacks.

1. Players are not properly positioned on the field.
2. Your players are not able to get rebound shots on the opposing team's goal.

Offense and Defense Drills
- **Drill 12.9: Center and Shoot.** Use this drill to teach your team how to center the ball. Getting the ball in front of the goal increases your scoring opportunities.
- **Drill 12.10: Corner Kick and Shoot.** This drill teaches your team how to properly execute a corner kick and how to defend against one. The principle of this drill is the same no matter how many players you use.
- **Drill 12.11: Throw-In and Shoot.** This drill teaches the throw-in. There are normally more throw-ins during a game than any other dead ball situation. Being able to gain an advantage with this skill is a must to win.
- **Drill 12.12: Goal Kick.** Goal kicks are comparable with throw-ins in the number performed during a game. Your team has to be able to clear the ball during a goal kick. Or, if the opposing team is kicking, your team must also be able to capture the ball.
- **Drill 12.13: Pass and Shoot.** This drill helps players make decisions on the field that result in passing the ball in order to move it down the field and create a shooting opportunity.

Formations

- **Drill 15.2: Position Play.** This is a drill that teaches through a controlled scrimmage.

If your players do not have proper shooting skills and techniques, they will only get one shot on goal. The other team's players will easily be able to capture the ball and get it out of the goal area to start its own attack on your goal.

Combination Shooting Drills

- **Drill 11.9: Triangle Pass and Shoot.** This drill is a combination of passing the ball one direction and then having the ball returned in the opposite direction to the shooter, who is now in a better position to shoot on goal.
- **Drill 11.10: Trail and Shoot.** This drill teaches players how to move the ball and to shadow the player with the ball to get a shooting opportunity.
- **Drill 11.11: Pass and Move.** This drill teaches passing, moving to open space, centering the ball, moving down the field, and shooting on goal. It covers everything that is necessary to properly perform in a game.
- **Drill 11.12: Flick and Move.** This drill teaches ball control, passing, and shooting on goal. While this is not an on-field move that is used often, it is helpful to develop touch on the ball and the ability to shoot on goal.
- **Drill 11.13: Drop and Shoot.** This drill teaches players to be aware of where they are on the field. It also requires communication with other players. It is a timing drill that uses passing, dribbling, and shooting.

Problem

My *players lose control of the ball* when it comes to them.

Solution

Many coaches don't put an emphasis on receiving the ball, and, as a result, the players can't gather the ball and maintain control.

1. All players must know how to receive the ball without it bouncing away from them.
2. Players must also know how to move to the ball, and away from the ball, to get into position to receive the ball from a teammate.

Offense and Defense Drills

- **Drill 12.2: Two on One.** This drill teaches players how to get the defense to commit, when to pass, and how to move to open space.
- **Drill 12.3: Two on Two.** This drill teaches players, offense and defense, to play as a team. It also requires the offensive players to move to keep the defense in a moving or chase position.
- **Drill 12.4: Three on Three.** This drill is as close to real game conditions as you can get. It requires the defensive players to work together and the offensive players to work together.
- **Drill 12.9: Center and Shoot.** Use this drill to teach your team how to center the ball. Getting the ball in front of the goal increases your scoring opportunities.
- **Drill 12.11: Throw-In and Shoot.** This drill teaches the throw-in. There are normally more throw-ins during a game than any other dead ball situation. Being able to gain an advantage is a must to win.
- **Drill 12.13: Pass and Shoot.** This drill allows your players to make decisions on the field that result in passing the ball down the field, creating a shooting opportunity.
- **Drill 12.14: Chip and Shoot.** This drill applies to all playing situations, and the skill can be performed during play or on a dead ball situation. Your players must be able to use the chip to advance the ball and create shooting opportunities.
- **Drill 12.16: Corner Kick Accuracy and Shoot.** Use this drill to improve the accuracy of the corner kick. It also helps your players learn to adjust on the ball coming from the kick.

Questions and Answers

This chapter answers the most common questions asked by coaches. These are not problems than can be entirely fixed with drills but are situations where knowledge can improve the play of your team. The information is in a question and answer format that allows you to find the question(s) you have and then read the answer to learn how to handle the situation.

Question

I play in an all-play league and have a few weak players on my team. Where can I play them where they will learn but not hurt the play of the rest of the team?

Answer

Every team has players that are less skilled than others. This is your chance to excel. All players want to be better, and they will listen and do what you want if they know they will learn and as a result be able to play more.

The best way is to identify your weakest players; then during the first half of each practice separate them and work on their deficiencies while you or your assistant coach works with the rest of the team. The one-on-one practice will enable the weaker players to advance faster.

The second half of the practice should be with the whole team. This practice will be the main emphasis of your practice. This is the fastest way to bring weaker players up to the level of your other players.

Where do you place them in the meanwhile? You should always have a substitute who can be moved into the fullbacks to give each of them a rest as they need it. You should have at least two substitutes for the halfbacks and one for the forwards. By putting your weaker players in and spacing them around the field, they will gain experience and you will not lose control of the game.

If you are putting in a weaker player at a halfback position, make sure you keep stronger players in at the fullback and forward positions. This will decrease the impact of the weaker player. The same is true no matter where you put the players. Surround them with stronger players.

Many coaches will put in all of their weaker players at the same time. This is just asking for problems. Develop a schedule of play that maximizes your assets.

Question

What is the best formation to use in a game?

Answer

When playing in small-sided games this is not normally a problem. However, when using a full 11 players this can be a problem. The most common formation for a team of 11 is the 4-3-3. All formations are counted starting with the fullbacks and moving forward. The goalkeeper is not included in the formation since all teams use a goalkeeper.

A 4-3-3 means four fullbacks, three halfbacks, and three forwards. This is a balanced formation, and it is easy to learn and easy to execute. Whatever formation you use, it must provide balance throughout the field.

Formations
- **Figure 15.3: 4-3-3 Formation.** This is the most commonly used formation because it provides strength throughout the entire field. It allows for a strong defense, midfield, and offense.
- **Figure 15.4: 4-4-2 Formation.** This formation is commonly used when the opposing team has a strong offense or when your team has gotten a good lead and you want to maintain the lead by providing more defense than offense. You will have a strong midfield and defense.

Question

How do I set up a schedule for practice?

Answer

Every practice should have three main components.

1. Warm-up, stretch, and ball control drills
2. Main emphasis drills to teach skills, techniques, and tactics
3. Cooldown period

Conditioning drills can be added during any portion of practice.

The main portion of your practice is usually determined by what happened in your last game. If the team did not pass well, then emphasize passing. If shooting was the problem, then stress shooting. You may end up with more than one area for each practice.

Using drills that capitalize on multiple skills are always the best.

Question

My team has numerous problems. Which problems do I work on first?

Answer

This is always a hard choice to make. However, if the team is lacking in most areas, start with the basics. Go to the assessment area of this book (Chapter 3) and evaluate your players. Then once you have a good idea of what area they are lacking the most in, go to the various drills chapters and pick out the drills that will teach those basic skills as well as related skills to improve other areas at the same time. There are many drills that combine skills. By choosing these drills you can increase your players' skill levels much faster than by just sticking with a single skill set.

If you have a team that lacks many of the basic skills, bringing players up to speed will take time, but you will notice improvements with each practice. Have patience and remember that they want to improve and will work hard if they believe you are there for them.

Question

How should I punish players for not listening or for goofing off?

Answer

This is a hard question to answer without knowing specifics, but generally positive reinforcement works better than any type of punishment. If you are running drills or doing something that has your players standing around for long periods of time waiting to do something, you are just encouraging them to misbehave.

You have to get them involved. The more involved they are the less chance of them acting out. If you have a player who is constantly misbehaving, take that player aside for a talk. Let that player know that his or her behavior is unacceptable. Explain that you want to be able to play him or her, but if the acting out continues, you will bench that person and use another player. Even if you are in an all-play league, you can contact league officials and let them know that you are going to discipline a player by not playing that person. Seldom will you ever have to go that far, but be prepared in case you do.

Another option is to talk to the player and the parents at the same time and let them know that the player's behavior is disruptive. This is not a preferred method, but the only other option is to remove the player from the team, and that doesn't help anyone.

Some coaches have players who misbehave run laps around the field. All this does is to get rid of the player for a short time. Running laps should never be used for discipline. It can be used for conditioning. If you want your team to run laps, that is fine and everyone should do it. Running laps while dribbling is even better.

Again, positive motivation is always the best. Point out to players the importance of conforming. Let them know what skills they have and how they can help the team. Let them know that they might be behaving badly, but they are not bad players. Many players act out to get attention. Positive attention will get them involved.

Question

What games or drills can I do with the team to reward them for their actions?

Answer

There are many fun drills that can be used to let players have fun and at the same time learn very valuable skills.

Fun Drills
- **Chapter 15: Position Play, Formations, and Fun Drills.** Volleyball/ Tennis, Juggling, Heading, and Throw-In are fun drills listed in Chapter 15. To the players it is just a fun time, but it requires skill and they will learn as they play. By using these fun drills you can reward your team and at the same time improve their skills.

Question

Do I need to do a warm-up prior to a game?

Answer

Yes. You should have a pregame routine that allows your team to warm-up, stretch their muscles, and get touches on the ball. A slow run around the field using leg lifts, for instance, is a start. Then a short series of stretches is next. After the stretches you can use multiple drills that enable players to gain the feel of the ball prior to starting the game.

Players who walk onto a field cold are not ready to play. They will be sluggish and may be slow to start. A simple pregame routine is important at every game.

Drills

- **Chapter 4: Warm-Up, Stretch, and Ball Control Drills.** Go to Chapter 4 and pick out the specific drills you want your team to do before the start of the game. Make it a routine so your players know what they will be doing each game. This saves time and makes them comfortable knowing what to expect. Using a small combination of warm-up, stretch, and ball control drills will get your team ready to play at kickoff. Many teams are sluggish at the start of the game. Give your team the edge by getting them warmed up and ready to go.

CHAPTER 8

Dribbling Drills

Coaching and training a soccer team without using drills is counterproductive. It is like going on vacation without knowing where you are going. You can't achieve your objectives if you don't have a plan to get there. A proper schedule coupled with the appropriate drills will provide success. Just going out to the practice field and playing soccer will not be as productive as having your players get more touches on the ball while they learn the necessary skills.

Don't misunderstand this message. Children love to play soccer and should be encouraged to do so. They can play soccer at any time, and this can be done without a coach. When they are at practice though, the practice should directly relate to the game of soccer and be fun for the players. All players will enjoy playing in a game more than practice, but if the practice is fun and they learn skills they can use in the game, they will also look forward to the practice.

Most of the drills in this chapter are combination drills. That means each drill covers more than one subset of skills. A dribbling drill might also use passing and shooting. While the main emphasis of the drill is on dribbling, the drill incorporates other subsets to make it more effective and realistic. The more drills you use that incorporate multiple skills, the better and faster your team will improve.

Drills

Basic Dribbling   (Figure 8.1)

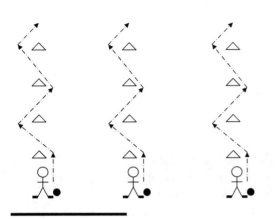

Figure 8.1
Basic Dribbling

Purpose: This drill teaches players proper dribbling technique.

Preparation: Set out cones to mark the dribbling course. Since you will have multiple lines of players, you will need duplicate courses of cones. Use four cones in each dribbling course.

Player needs: Each player needs a ball.

Drill execution: This is the simplest dribbling drill you can do other than just dribbling in a straight line without cones. The players can dribble at their own speeds to develop control and learn to move the ball right and left, or you can advance the skill level by pitting teams of players against each other. Each player starts at the closest cone and dribbles around the cones using the insteps of their feet to move the ball right or left.

Coaching Tips

1. Watch players as they move the ball right or left. Players should keep the ball in front of them, and, as a result, they must use the insteps of their feet to redirect the ball left or right.

2. Check that your players are not just watching the ball. They should keep their heads up to see the upcoming cones and maneuver around them.

3. Watch to see that all dribbling, straight, right, or left, is done with balance. Players should move with even strides and not have to take multiple extra steps, or stutter steps, to control the ball.

Dribbling with Cone   (Figure 8.2)

Purpose: This drill teaches players to dribble with their heads up so they can see the field.

Preparation: Set out cones to mark the dribbling course. Since you will have multiple lines of players, you will need duplicate courses of cones. Use four cones in each dribbling course. Also gather saucer cones for each player or for as many players as you have cones.

Player needs: Each player needs a ball plus one saucer cone.

Drill execution: Players dribble through the cones using the insteps of their feet in order to redirect the ball right or left. Place a saucer cone on the head of each player. If cones fall off during the dribbling drill, have players pick them up, put them back on their heads, and continue. If you do not have enough saucer cones for everyone on the team, gather saucer cones from the players who have completed the drill and give them to players just starting the drill.

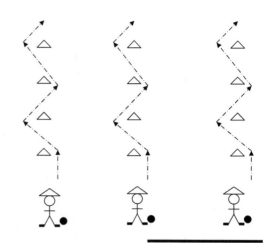

Figure 8.2
Dribbling with Cone

Coaching Tips

1. Be sure players have their heads up. If players are dribbling with their heads up, the cones will not fall off. If they are looking down at the ball, the cones will fall off. Don't let players put the cones on the back of their heads so they can look down while dribbling.

2. Watch for ball control, balance, and the ability to dribble with the head up. This is important to learn. If players just look at the ball, they will be unable to see open space or other players around the field.

3. Repeat this drill as required to teach the players to dribble without staring at the ball.

Reverse the Ball Dribble (Figure 8.3)

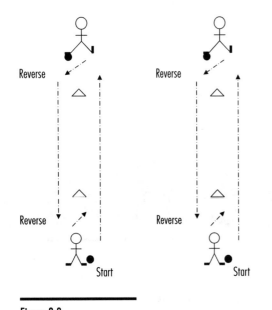

Figure 8.3
Reverse the Ball Dribble

Purpose: This drill teaches players how to reverse the ball while dribbling.

Preparation: Set up two cones for each player. Use enough cones so half the team can perform the drill at the same time. The cones should be spaced approximately 10 to 15 feet apart.

Player needs: Each player needs a ball.

Drill execution: Each player dribbles to the farthest cone. As the player passes the cone, he or she uses the outside of the foot to reverse or redirect the ball and then dribble back to the starting cone. Players go beyond that cone and, using the opposite foot they used for the first cone, they again redirect and reverse the ball to return to the starting cone. At that time the next player starts the drill. Start the drill approximately five steps from the first cone.

Coaching Tips

1. Be sure each player uses the correct foot. To turn the ball the player needs to use the outside of the foot. If using the right foot to turn the ball, the toe of the right foot will be pointing to the right and the player will push the ball with the outside middle of the foot. When using the left foot, the toe of the left foot will be pointing to the left and the player will push with the outside of the left foot to reverse the ball.

2. See that players maintain their balance throughout the drill, even when redirecting and reversing the ball.

3. Make sure players do not just watch the ball. They can glance at the ball but must still be able to keep their heads up to see where they are going.

Change Speed Dribbling   (Figure 8.4)

Purpose: This drill teaches players how to vary their speed while dribbling. This type of technique is a necessity for playing soccer.

Preparation: Have four cones for each player. Make multiple lines to allow more players to do the drill. Stagger the cones so that there are 5 steps between the first and second cones, 10 steps between the second and third cones, and 5 steps between the third and fourth cones.

Player needs: Each player needs to have a ball.

Drill execution: Have each player running the drill start with a slow dribble. When the player reaches the second cone, he or she picks up speed and dribbles fast. At the third cone, the player again slows down, goes around the end cone, and then goes fast to the first cone, slow to the next cone, and fast to the finish. At every cone the player will change speed. When the player finishes the drill, have the player stop the ball by placing a foot on top of the ball and reversing it to get back to the starting cone.

Add to drill: After you have run this drill to get players comfortable with changing speed, insert a defender. Start at midfield and have the player with the ball dribble toward the goal, changing speed as he or she moves down the field. The player can stop the ball and start again or just change speed to throw off the defender by keeping the defender guessing and off balance. When there is an open shot on the goal, the first player shoots.

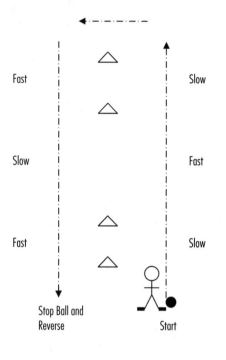

Figure 8.4
Change Speed Dribbling

Coaching Tips

1. Be sure all players can change speed while dribbling. This is a must, as it puts the dribbler in control of the situation and does not let the defender get control.

2. Watch your players to make sure they maintain control while dribbling fast and slow.

3. Watch the turn to ensure that the player utilizes a proper reverse movement.

4. When the player finishes the dribbling, he or she should stop the ball by placing a foot on the ball and then pulling it back to bring the ball back to the starting cone. All movements should be accomplished while the player maintains control and balance.

Step Over Right/Left Dribbling (Figure 8.5)

Purpose: This drill teaches players how to move the ball to the left and right while faking out the defense.

Preparation: Using four cones, place them in a square with each about 10 steps apart. Set up multiple sets of cones so you can have multiple players running the drill at the same time.

Player needs: Each player needs a ball.

Drill execution: The player with the ball dribbles to the first cone. Stopping directly in front of the cone, the player stops the ball, steps over the ball with the right foot, and then kicks the ball to the right with the outside of the foot. The player then dribbles to the next cone and repeats the movement. Players will continue until they have reached the starting cone.

When the last player at each drill area finishes, repeat the drill, but this time have them go counterclockwise around the cones, using their left foot to step over the ball and then push the ball to the left.

Add to drill: Once everyone is able to redirect the ball by using the fake movement to redirect the ball, place a defender on the penalty box outer line and have the player with the ball dribble to that defender. When the dribbling player gets to the defender, make the step right/left move to get around the defender. Even though the defender will know what the dribbling player is going to do, that player will be able to use step movement. The player can step over and push the ball left or right, or do a double — stepping over and then stepping back without moving the ball. The player can then continue by moving the ball with the instep of the foot.

Stop in front
of the cone.

Step over the ball and kick
with the outside of the foot
used to step over the ball.

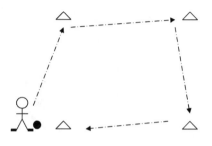

Figure 8.5

Step Over
Right/Left Dribbling

Coaching Tips

1. Make sure the player goes directly to the cone since the cone represents a defender.

2. Watch that players are centered on the ball, a requirement to do this movement properly.

3. Ensure the player makes the move quickly. Speed is necessary to initiate this fake.

Fake Kick Dribbling   (Figure 8.6)

Purpose: This is a fake kick done while dribbling. This move often freezes the defender, allowing the player with the ball to move around that player.

Preparation: Set three cones in a straight line approximately 10 feet apart. Use multiple lines so you can have multiple players doing the drill at the same time. Have each player start at the first cone and then perform the drill using the second and third cone.

Player needs: Each player needs a ball.

Drill execution: Have each player dribble directly in front of the cone. After reaching the cone, the player stops and then fakes a kick. The player does this by drawing back the leg as if to kick, but instead of kicking the player uses the step over right/left move, described in the previous drill, to move to open space where he or she is free to actually shoot. Each player will fake the kick at each cone and then dribble around the last cone and repeat the movements on the return to the starting cone.

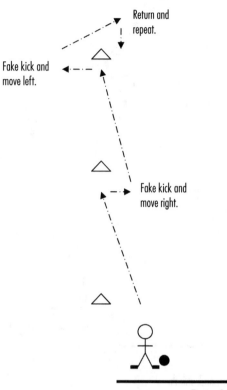

Figure 8.6
Fake Kick Dribbling

Coaching Tips

1. See that players approach the cone so they are centered on it.

2. Be sure the player stops the ball and fakes a kick. It must be realistic to actually fake out the defender. Once they have frozen the defender, they move right or left to get an open shot.

3. Be sure that after the fake, the player moves to the right or left and continues dribbling to the next cone.

4. Watch for proper movement while dribbling, stopping, fake kicking, and moving the ball to the right or left.

Turn and Dribble   (Figure 8.7)

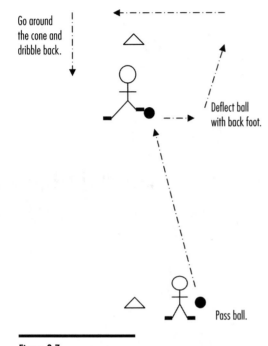

Go around
the cone and
dribble back.

Deflect ball
with back foot.

Pass ball.

Figure 8.7
Turn and Dribble

Purpose: This drill teaches players to reverse a ball that is coming straight to them from the front.

Preparation: Set two cones approximately 10 steps apart in a straight line. This drill requires two players, one player to pass the ball and one player to receive and turn the ball. Set up two cones for each team of players you have doing the drill.

Player needs: Every team of two players needs one ball.

Drill execution: The player at the starting cone passes the ball to the second player, who will be standing in front of the second cone. While the ball is coming, the second player centers on the ball. When centered on the ball, the player will move one leg to the rear of the body. As the ball approaches, the player moves the left or right foot back behind the body line. This is the leg used to deflect the ball. The toe of this foot will be pointing away from the body. The player lets the ball pass the center of his or her body and then lets the ball deflect off the back foot, which is pointed out to deflect the ball to the outside. This moves the ball to the outside. If the left foot is used to deflect the ball, it should move to the left. The right foot will move the ball right. This movement will allow the player to move past a defender without stopping the ball. The player then moves to the ball and dribbles back to the starting line. The player who passed the ball will now move out into the field, and another player will step forward and pass the ball to the new player.

Coaching Tips

1. Make sure the player passing the ball uses proper passing techniques.

2. See that players receiving the ball move to center on it.

3. Make sure the back foot that is used to deflect the ball is pointing away from the player's body.

4. When the ball has been deflected, ensure the player moves to the ball quickly.

Conclusion Drill

Combine Drills 8.1–8.7 into a simple drill. Have each of your players dribble against a defender, using the different dribbling techniques. Each player should be able to vary speed, fake right or left, turn back, stop the ball and actually move right or left, or fake a kick. Make sure players use at least three of these movements each time they do the drill. Start at the half line, and have the player with the ball move toward the goal. Since the defender will not know what movement the offensive player is going to use, the player with the ball will get a full understanding of what can be accomplished with the different movements.

CHAPTER 9

Passing Drills

When learning passing drills your players have to learn the proper skills and techniques in steps. You have to learn how to pass before you can pass effectively.

The first step is to learn the fundamentals of passing, which includes learning how to pass accurately. This step is done while players are stationary. In other words, players pass the ball from a standing position without running. Proper technique and accuracy form the foundation of being a good passer.

The second step consists of knowing when to pass and being able to pass while moving. Holding the ball until a defender has committed or another player is open is essential to the game of soccer. So is the ability to make a pass that goes to where the player is, not to where the player was. The pass must lead so the player receiving the pass doesn't have to change direction or speed. Training both of these steps will make your team a highly efficient passing team, and a highly efficient passing team is almost impossible to stop. It will be able to move the ball anywhere on the field.

Drills

Ball on Cone   (Figure 9.1)

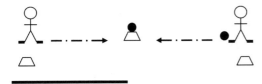

Figure 9.1
Ball on Cone

Purpose: Accuracy is a must in passing. This drill teaches players proper passing techniques as well as accuracy.

Preparation: Set three saucer cones in a straight line. The cones should be approximately 10 steps from each other.

Player needs: Each drill team consists of two players and two balls. The two players use the three saucer cones.

Drill execution: Place one ball on top of the center saucer cone. Each player will stand at one of the two outside cones. The second ball is placed on the ground next to an outside cone. One player will start the drill by standing still and passing the ball toward the ball sitting on the center cone. The object is to knock the ball off the cone. The players will keep track of how many times they knock off the ball. This is done by using all of your players competing against each other. To do this drill, a player stands beside the ball with his or her plant foot stationary and passes the ball by moving his or her other foot through the ball. Players should use both feet to pass. Let players know when it is time to change passing feet.

Add to drill: After you have done this drill and the players are using the proper part of the foot and their accuracy has increased, have them move back one step. This time they will be doing the same drill but will be stepping to the ball, placing the plant foot next to the ball and then striking the ball to pass it. This is a progression from standing next to the ball to stepping up to the ball.

Coaching Tips

1. Observe the player's balance over the ball and whether he or she is striking the ball with the instep.

2. Watch for follow-through on the pass.

3. Emphasize proper passing and accuracy.

Pass to Player (Figure 9.2)

Purpose: This drill teaches players to pass to teammates. They learn to pass to their right, left, and front.

Preparation: Place four players in a diamond formation. If you do not have an even amount of players, you can use three players in a triangle formation. Place players so they are approximately 5 to 10 yards apart from each other.

Player needs: Each team of three or four players needs one ball.

Drill execution: While stationary, players pass to the other players. Start by passing the ball in a clockwise direction. Then have players pass in a counterclockwise direction. The next step is to pass across to the other players, letting the passers decide where and to whom the ball will be passed.

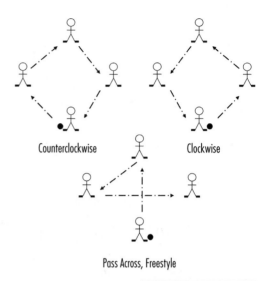

Counterclockwise   Clockwise

Pass Across, Freestyle

Figure 9.2
Pass to Player

Coaching Tips

1. Monitor your players for proper passing technique and for accuracy. The players they are passing to should not have to move very much to receive the ball.

2. Make sure players receiving the ball move to center themselves on the ball.

3. Observe the proper receiving techniques. The player should be able to receive the ball without kicking it away. The ball should stay within that player's control zone, an area where the player receiving the ball has control of the ball, not an opposing player.

4. Check that passes are sharp. The ball should travel directly to the other player and not just roll up very slowly.

Pass to Moving Player Through Goal (Figure 9.3)

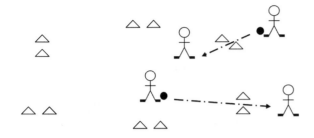

Figure 9.3

Pass to Moving Player
Through Goal

Purpose: This drill improves passing accuracy while moving, communication among players, and support.

Preparation: Set up two cones to make one goal. Place six to eight goals around the field. The spacing between the two cones that form a goal should be one yard. The goals can be placed anywhere.

Player needs: Each team of two players needs one ball.

Drill execution: Have the player with the ball start dribbling. The player without the ball will point to a goal and then go to the back of the goal. The player with the ball will pass the ball through the goal to the partner. When the partner receives the ball, the player that passed it will call out and point to another goal. The team will move to that goal, pass the ball through, and continue. The players can go to any goal; there is no set direction or rotation.

Coaching Tips

1. Make sure the two players are talking to each other and are moving as a team.

2. Watch to be sure the dribbling player has his or her head up to see the other player and the goal.

3. Make sure the player receiving the ball moves in front of the ball and doesn't chase the ball after it is passed through the goal.

4. Check that the players on the field don't get grouped up and are able to move to an open goal.

5. Watch your players to make sure they are passing properly and are receiving properly.

Rock 'Em Sock 'Em Passing   (Figure 9.4)

Purpose: This drill is great to teach players when to pass. Many players hold the ball too long or pass before it's appropriate. This drill teaches timing and the necessity for passing accuracy. This drill will also teach your players proper decision making. They will learn how much time they have to pass, how to make an opponent commit, and how to pass with accuracy.

Preparation: Break players into groups of five to eight.

Player needs: One ball and one long tube sock are needed for each playing group.

Drill execution: Designate one player as the "SOCK ER." Give this player the tube sock. Give one of the other players in the group the ball. The object is to try and tag the player with the ball, using the sock, before that player can pass. The player with the sock can move anywhere and can tag the player passing or the player receiving the ball. When the player with the sock tags another player before that player can get rid of the ball, the first player changes place with the tagged player, who now has the sock.

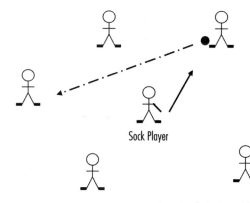

Sock Player

Figure 9.4
Rock 'Em Sock 'Em Passing

Coaching Tips

1. Make sure the player with the ball holds the ball until the player with the sock is committed to tagging him or her.

2. Watch to be sure that once the player with the sock is committed, the player with the ball passes to another player. This does not allow the player with the sock to play anyone other than the player with the ball.

3. Make sure the ball is passed directly to another player rather than just kicking it to get rid of the ball.

4. Watch the player receiving the ball. That player can do a control dribble or a one-touch pass if the sock player is near. Look for good decision making.

Wall Pass   (Figure 9.5)

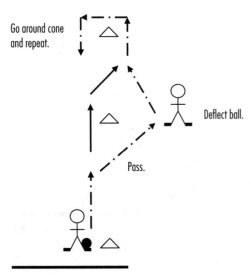

Go around cone
and repeat.

Deflect ball.

Pass.

Figure 9.5
Wall Pass

Purpose: The wall pass is a very effective method for moving around an opponent while maintaining control of the ball. This drill teaches the basics of working with a teammate to move past an opponent.

Preparation: Set three cones in a straight line with 10 yards between each of them. Set up multiple lines so you can have several teams doing the drill at the same time. Break players into teams of two.

Player needs: Each team of two players needs one ball.

Drill execution: Place one player at one side of the center cone, which is representing a player from the other team. The second player will dribble toward that cone. When the player with the ball is near the cone, that player will pass to the person standing beside the cone. The player receiving the ball will deflect the ball so it goes behind the cone. The player that originally passed the ball will go around the cone, pick up the ball, and dribble. This player dribbles around the next cone and comes back, repeating the process. All the player in the center has to do is turn so he or she is always facing the player dribbling the ball. Rotate players each time. The player in the center goes to the end of the line, and the player who just dribbled becomes the player deflecting the ball.

Coaching Tips

1. Watch that the player with the ball uses proper dribbling techniques.

2. Make sure the pass is to the center player. If it is not, make sure the player receiving the ball moves in front of the ball.

3. Check that the player in the center deflects the ball without stopping it and then passing. This will move the ball quickly around the cone (i.e., the opposing player).

4. Start this drill at a slow pace, and then pick up the speed as your players gain efficiency.

Pass Between Cones   (Figure 9.6)

Purpose: This drill teaches the short pass as well as passing and receiving with both feet.

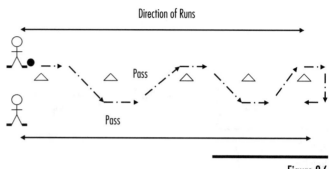

Preparation: Set up five cones in a straight line, approximately five yards apart. You can set up multiple rows to allow more players to run the drill at the same time. There are two players for each line of cones. Stand one player on each side of the cones.

Figure 9.6
Pass Between Cones

Player needs: Each team of two players needs one ball.

Drill execution: Have the player with the ball start to dribble. After passing the first cone, that player passes the ball to the other player. That player controls the ball and dribbles to the next cone where he or she passes. The players will continue passing until they reach the last cone. There they turn and continue passing between the cones as they return to the starting point.

Coaching Tips

1. Ensure that your players are using proper passing and receiving techniques.

2. Make sure players pass with their outside feet using their insteps. Players receiving the ball should also use their outside feet so the ball will be controlled and stay in front of them.

3. Watch for the touch on the ball. The pass should be soft enough to reach the player and should lead the player so that he or she does not have to stop or speed up to get the ball.

4. Be sure that on the first leg of the drill, the player on the left receives and passes the ball using the left foot. The player on the right will be using the right foot for receiving and passing. On the reverse trip, each player will be using the foot opposite the one used before. This teaches players to use both feet.

5. To make this more fun, have teams compete against each other.

Drop Pass   (Figure 9.7)

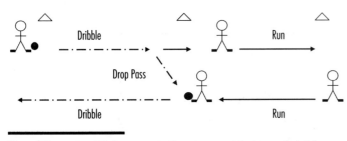

Figure 9.7
Drop Pass

Purpose: This drill teaches players how to work together to drop off a pass to another player moving in the opposite direction.

Preparation: Use three cones spaced approximately 10 steps apart in a straight line. Set up multiple lines, so numerous players can do the drill at the same time.

Player needs: Each team of two players needs one ball.

Drill execution: Place one player at each end cone. Have the player with the ball start dribbling toward the middle cone. As this player starts dribbling, the player on the opposite side of the field starts running toward the dribbling player. When the player with the ball gets approximately four or five steps from the other player, the player with the ball pushes the ball out, using the outside of the foot, so the ball goes into the path of the player approaching. That player will gain control of the ball and continue dribbling to the cone. The two players then turn and repeat the action. If you are using more than one group on each set of cones, let each player go both directions and then change teams.

Coaching Tips

1. Make sure the player with the ball uses proper dribbling techniques.

2. When "dropping off" the ball to the other player, make sure that the player passing the ball does not kick it at the approaching player but lays it off so the approaching player can pick up the ball without losing control.

3. Listen for players communicating with each other.

4. Watch that when the ball is passed, it is in front of the player and not to the side. If the pass is not good, make sure the player receiving the ball goes to the ball.

5. Look for a smooth drop of the ball, which will enable your team to reverse the direction of the ball without losing control.

Reverse Pass   (Figure 9.8)

Purpose: This pass teaches players to reverse the ball while on a full run.

Preparation: Use three cones spaced approximately 10 steps apart in a straight line. Set up multiple lines so numerous players can do the drill at the same time.

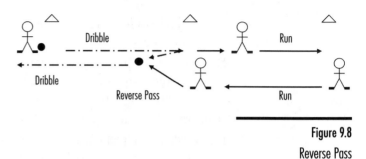

Figure 9.8

Reverse Pass

Player needs: Have one ball per two players.

Drill execution: Place one player at each end cone. The player with the ball starts dribbling toward the middle cone. At the same time, the player on the opposite side of the field starts running toward that player. When the player with the ball gets approximately four or five steps from the other player, the player with the ball places a foot on top of the ball and rolls it backward, using the bottom of the foot. The ball should go behind that player and into the path of the player approaching. That player will gain control of the ball and dribble back to the cone. The two players then turn and repeat the action. If you are using more than one group on each set of cones, let each player go both directions and then change teams.

Coaching Tips

1. Make sure the player with the ball uses proper dribbling techniques.

2. When reversing the ball to pass to the approaching player, make sure that the player passing the ball places a foot on top of the ball and directs it backward so it goes near the path of the approaching player. The ball should roll backward, and the player approaching should adjust to be directly in front of the ball. The approaching player should pick up the ball without losing control.

3. Make sure players communicate with each other.

4. Check that when the ball is reversed, it rolls in front of the player and not to the side. If the pass is not good, make sure the player receiving the ball goes to the ball.

5. Watch for a smooth reverse of the ball, which will enable your team to reverse the direction of the ball without losing control.

Reverse Pass Team Competition   (Figure 9.9)

Purpose: This is a team activity that teaches the reverse pass, balance, coordination, and teamwork.

Preparation: Split players into two teams. Use four cones for each team, and place them in an evenly spaced straight line with approximately 10 steps between each cone.

Player needs: Each team needs one ball.

Drill execution: The first player in line will take off dribbling the ball. When that player reaches the third cone, he or she rolls the ball back. The second player, who is running behind the first player, cannot go beyond the second cone until the first player has passed back. That second player then dribbles the ball from the second to third cone and passes back. This will be repeated with each player on the team. After passing the ball back, the player will run on to the end cone and get ready to repeat the drill from the opposite direction.

The last player in line picks up the reverse pass and dribbles to the front player. That last player then rolls the ball back, and the first player in line starts again.

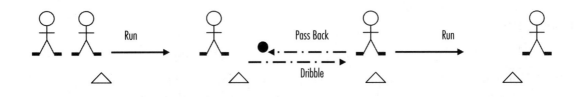

Figure 9.9   Reverse Pass Team Competition

Coaching Tips

1. Make this a competition after the players have learned to do the reverse pass and it will increase their accuracy and skill. They will quickly learn that if they make bad passes they will not win.

2. Make sure that the trailing player does not pass the second cone until the ball is passed back.

3. Do not let the players use their heels. They should reverse the ball using the bottom of the foot.

4. Use this fun drill to help your players improve their dribbling and passing skills and develop cardiovascular endurance.

Pass Through Legs (Figure 9.10)

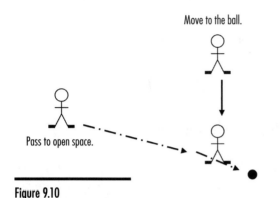

Move to the ball.

Pass to open space.

Figure 9.10
Pass Through Legs

Purpose: The ability to pass to the feet of another player is a must in soccer. This drill teaches players the proper place to pass.

Preparation: No cones are needed for this drill. Let your players move anywhere they want on your practice field.

Player needs: Separate the players into teams of two. One soccer ball is needed for each team.

Drill execution: Have the player with the ball pass to open space on the field. The other player will move to center on the ball. That player will then position himself or herself on the ball and let the ball roll through the legs. After the ball has gone through the legs, that player turns, gets the ball, and then passes to open space, at which time the other player will move to the ball.

Coaching Tips

1. Make sure the player passing the ball uses the proper passing techniques.

2. Check that the player passing the ball passes it into open space, but close enough for the other player to be able to reach the ball while the ball is still rolling.

3. Watch that the player receiving the pass moves to the ball and centers on the ball. This teaches the proper way to receive a pass. The ball should be moving and roll through the legs.

4. Be sure players are in constant motion and do not stop.

CHAPTER 10

Shooting Drills

Your team must be able to shoot the ball and place it into the goal. Many teams find they can move the ball to an opponent's goal but are unable to put the ball into the goal. Most of the time the failure to score is a lack of confidence by the players in their ability to shoot the ball. Often players hesitate, losing their chance to score.

These drills will help players develop confidence, but you as a coach must emphasize that they have to shoot. It is better to shoot and miss than not to shoot at all. Players cannot score if they don't shoot.

Drills

Shooting with Cone   (Figures 10.1, 10.2, and 10.3)

Purpose: This drill uses three steps to teach the proper way to kick the ball to have an effective shot. These are the first steps in teaching your players to shoot.

Preparation: Use a goal or set up cones to mark the perimeters of the goal. Set up a saucer cone for each player. Place the cones in front of the goal, approximately 10 steps from the goal and about 1 step apart.

Kick with the plant foot next to the ball.

Figure 10.1
Stationary Kick

Player needs: Each player will need a ball to place on the cone.

Drill execution: This drill is done in three steps.

First step—Stationary Kick (Figure 10.1): Have each player place his or her ball on top of the saucer cone. Standing with the plant foot next to the ball, each player kicks the ball. Since the ball is elevated off of the ground, it is easy for the player to use the laces on the shoes.

Coaching Tips

1. Make sure players use the laces on their shoes to strike the ball.

2. Watch for proper follow-through after players strike the ball. The kick action should not stop at the ball but should go through the ball.

3. Make sure the plant foot is pointing in the direction of the goal.

Second step — One Step and Kick (Figure 10.2): Have each player take one step back from the ball on the cone. Have players step up to the balls with their plant feet and kick the balls off of the cones toward the goal.

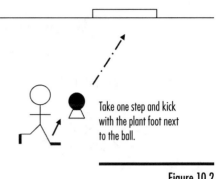

Take one step and kick with the plant foot next to the ball.

Figure 10.2
One Step and Kick

Coaching Tips

1. Check the plant foot to ensure the toe is pointing toward the goal.

2. Be sure each player is balanced over the ball.

3. Watch to ensure the ball is struck with the laces of the shoe and that the motion of the kick goes through the ball.

Third step — Run and Kick (Figure 10.3): Move your players back two or three steps and have them run to their balls and kick while on the move.

Run to the ball and kick with the plant foot next to the ball.

Figure 10.3
Run and Kick

Coaching Tips

1. Watch to ensure the players are centered on the ball and have the plant foot in a proper position for shooting the ball.

2. Check that players are balanced and able to put some power into the shot.

3. Again, check that the ball is struck with the laces of the shoe and there is a proper follow-through.

4. After the kick, make sure the player follows the ball toward the goal and does not stop after the shot.

Shooting with Both Feet (Figure 10.4)

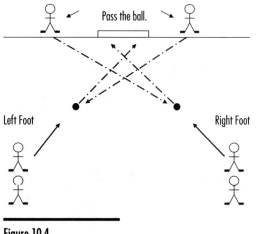

Figure 10.4
Shooting with Both Feet

Purpose: This drill teaches players how to adjust to a ball coming to them from an angle and to shoot with one touch on the ball using both feet.

Preparation: Use a goal, or set up cones to mark the perimeter of a goal. Position a player on each side of the goal and on the end line. Line up the remainder of your players outside the penalty box. They will be in two lines, facing the goal. Place your goalkeeper in the goal.

Player needs: The players on the end line, who will be passing the ball, need numerous balls to pass.

Drill execution: Start with one of the players on the end line passing the ball out into the field and across the face of the goal. The first player in line on the opposite side of the goal from the passer will move forward, center on the ball and the goal, and shoot using one touch. As soon as the player has shot, that player goes to the end line and replaces the player that passed to him or her. The player who was replaced will go to the end of one of the lines on the field. After the first player has cleared the goal, the player on the opposite side of the goal will pass the ball across the field and the player on the opposite side will then shoot.

Keep this rotation and the ball moving. The goalkeeper will catch the ball if possible; if not, the goalkeeper will collect the ball and roll it to the side to a player passing the ball. If the ball misses the goal area, the player that shot the ball gets it. The player approaching from the right side will shoot with the right foot, and the player approaching from the left side will shoot with the left foot. Make sure your players alternate from the right to left lines.

Coaching Tips

1. As the player taking the shot approaches the ball, make sure that player is centered on the ball and the goal so he or she is able to shoot while on balance.

2. Check that the shot is from one touch. If it is a bad pass and the player has to control the ball, make sure the shot is done quickly after control is gained.

3. Watch that the player approaching on the right side of the goal uses the right foot to shoot while the player approaching from the left side uses the left foot to shoot.

4. Make sure players shooting the ball keep their eyes on the ball until they have kicked it.

5. Be sure that after the kick, the player follows the ball into the goal. If the goalkeeper drops the ball or the ball bounces back, have the player take a second shot.

6. Make sure this is a fast-moving drill. Do not let your players stand around.

7. Watch to ensure the goalkeeper moves with the ball to reduce the angle of the shot.

Catch the Ball and Shoot   (Figure 10.5)

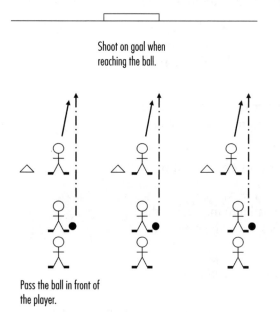

Shoot on goal when reaching the ball.

Pass the ball in front of the player.

Figure 10.5
Catch the Ball and Shoot

Purpose: This drill teaches players to communicate, to quickly pick up the ball as it comes from behind, and to take a quick shot on goal.

Preparation: Use a goal, or set up cones to mark the perimeter of the goal. Break your players into teams of three players each. Put the first player on the penalty box line with the remaining two players behind him or her in a straight line. Mark the position of each line with a cone. Put your goalkeeper in the goal area.

Player needs: Each player needs a ball.

Drill execution: Have the first player in each line move forward four or five steps. This player will be facing the goal with the back to the player passing the ball. The second player in line will yell "ball," and then that player will pass the ball so it goes beyond the first player. The first player will run to the ball and shoot on goal. That player will then collect the ball and return to the line.

Coaching Tips

1. Make sure the players communicate with each other to know when and where the ball is being passed.

2. Check that the player kicking the ball goes to the ball and centers on the ball to take the shot on goal.

3. Make sure the player passing the ball uses proper passing techniques.

4. After the player shoots on goal, make sure the player follows the ball to get a chance for a second, or follow-up, shot.

Turn and Shoot   (Figure 10.6)

Purpose: This drill teaches players to shoot while moving across the face of the goal.

Preparation: Use a goal, or set up cones to mark the perimeter of the goal. Place two cones in front of the goal. Position them so they are outside the goalposts. Split the team into two groups. One group lines up on the right side and the other group on the left side of the cones. You do not need a goalkeeper for this drill since two players will be shooting at the same time.

Player needs: Each player needs a ball.

Drill execution: Have a player from each side dribble toward the cones placed near the goalposts. As players pass their cones, have them turn and shoot on goal. After they shoot have them follow their balls into the goal, collect their balls, and move to the opposite side and get back into line. The player moving from the left side will shoot with the right foot, and the player moving from the right side will shoot with the left foot.

Coaching Tips

1. Make sure players dribble to the cone, turn the ball, and then shoot as soon as they have control. It is a must to shoot quickly.

2. Watch that each player uses the proper foot to shoot and does not position the ball for a particular foot.

3. Be sure the player follows the ball into the goal after the shot.

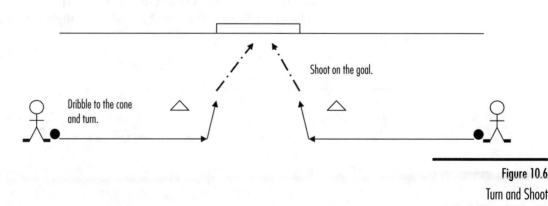

Figure 10.6
Turn and Shoot

Redirect the Ball Shooting   (Figure 10.7)

Purpose: This drill teaches players how to properly redirect or deflect the ball. This is an effective method of scoring.

Preparation: Use a goal, or set up cones to mark the perimeter of the goal. Two players will do each drill, one to pass and one to shoot. Mark the starting points of each player with cones. The cone for the shooter should be about five steps beyond the far post of the player passing. The player passing should be approximately 10 steps from the near post of the goal.

Player needs: The player passing needs a ball.

Drill execution: Have the player pass the ball across the front of the goal. The player shooting on the goal moves to center on the ball and then stops and, using the outside foot, redirects the ball into the goal. After the player shoots, that player moves to the passing line and the player who passed moves to the shooting line. Keep the players moving so they rotate quickly.

Coaching Tips

1. Make sure the player shooting centers on the ball and stops to deflect the ball.

2. Observe if a player uses the foot farthest from the goal to deflect the ball.

3. Make sure each player turns the deflection foot so the ball changes direction and goes into the goal. A player does this by turning the toe of the deflection foot to the outside so it is at a 45-degree angle away from the goal.

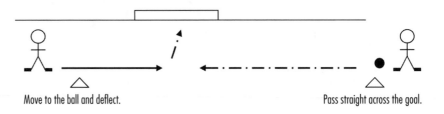

Move to the ball and deflect.   Pass straight across the goal.

Figure 10.7

Redirect the Ball Shooting

CHAPTER 11

Combination Shooting Drills

Once players have a grasp of the basics of shooting, it is time to start working on shooting methods they will use in the game. The combination shooting drills in this chapter use passing, moving to open space, heading, throw-ins, and other techniques to prepare your players for actual game situations.

Combination drills are the best and fastest way to get your team trained. When you combine multiple skills into a drill you end up with your players learning more than with a single point drill. Single point drills are necessary to learn a basic skill, but once the skill is learned moving on to combination drills is a must.

Throw-In/Heading and Shooting Drills

Head and Shoot   (Figure 11.1)

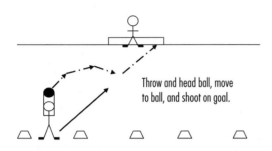

Throw and head ball, move
to ball, and shoot on goal.

Figure 11.1
Head and Shoot

Purpose: This is an individual drill during which each player heads the ball and then moves to the ball and shoots on goal. This drill teaches heading, moving to the ball, and shooting on goal.

Preparation: Use a goal, or set up cones to mark the perimeter of the goal. Line up the players on the penalty box line. Mark this line with saucer cones.

Player needs: Each player needs a ball.

Drill execution: Line up your players side by side on the penalty box line. They will be facing the goal. One at a time, have each player throw the ball into the air and then head the ball forward toward the goal. As soon as a player heads the ball, have that player move to the ball and shoot with one touch.

Coaching Tips

1. Watch players to ensure they use proper heading techniques.

2. Make sure players head the ball forward toward the goal.

3. Check that your players move to the ball as soon as they head the ball.

4. Remember the shot should be with one touch. Don't let players dribble. They shoot when they reach the ball.

Head to Shooter (Figure 11.2)

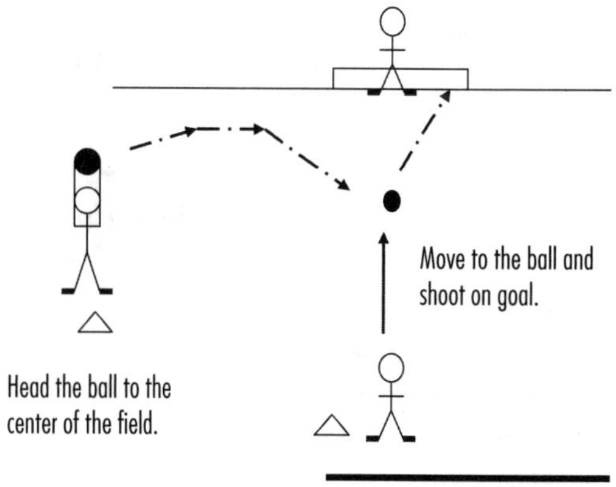

Purpose: This drill involves heading, moving to the ball by another player, and shooting on goal.

Preparation: Use a goal, or set up cones to mark the perimeter of the goal. You need two cones, one to mark where the player stands to head the ball and one where the player shooting the ball starts from.

Player needs: The player heading the ball will need a ball.

Drill execution: Place one player next to the cone directly in front of the goal. This cone should be approximately 15 steps in front of the goal. The remaining players will be at the cone that is to the side of the goal. This cone should be approximately 10 steps from the nearest goalpost and approximately halfway between the end line and the center cone.

Move to the ball and shoot on goal.

Head the ball to the center of the field.

Figure 11.2
Head to Shooter

Start play by having the player at the side cone head the ball into the center of the field. As soon as the player throws the ball into the air to head it, the player in the center runs toward the goal. As that player runs, he or she adjusts to the position of the ball and shoots with one touch on the ball. After the player shoots, the player that headed the ball moves to the center cone and becomes the next shooter.

Coaching Tips

1. Make sure the player heading the ball throws the ball high enough to get distance on the ball.

2. Watch for proper movement of the player to get the correct heading of the ball.

3. Ensure the player shooting the ball watches the player heading the ball and moves when the ball is thrown into the air.

4. The player shooting the ball should move to the ball, get centered, and shoot without dribbling. The shot should be quick and accurate.

Run to Goal Heading (Figure 11.3)

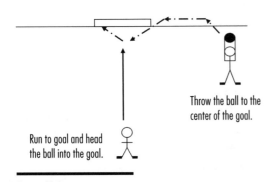

Throw the ball to the
center of the goal.

Run to goal and head
the ball into the goal.

Figure 11.3
Run to Goal Heading

Purpose: This drill develops the accuracy and strength necessary to direct the ball into the goal while on the move.

Preparation: Use a goal, or set up cones to mark the perimeter of the goal. You may or may not use the goalkeeper to do this drill. Split your team into two lines.

Player needs: Put all of the soccer balls with the group of players throwing the balls.

Drill execution: Line up half the team in front, facing the goal. They should be lined up on the penalty box line. Have the other half of the team line up at the side of the goal, approximately five steps out from the end line. Have a player run toward the goal, and have the player on the side do a throw-in that goes up in the air. The player running in has to adjust to the ball and head the ball into the goal. After this has been done a few times by all players, move the thrower to the opposite side of the goal and repeat the drill with the ball coming from the opposite direction.

Coaching Tips

1. Make sure the player running in watches the player throwing the ball and, when the ball is thrown, adjusts to center on the ball.

2. Ensure the player throwing in the ball places the ball in front of the approaching player and at the correct distance. Accuracy of the throw-in is a must.

3. Watch to ensure that the player heading the ball moves to the ball and then uses proper heading techniques to place the ball into the goal. The ball should be placed to the right or left side of the goal.

Side Heading (Figure 11.4)

Purpose: This drill teaches players to head the ball to the left or right corners of the goal while running straight on the ball.

Preparation: Use a goal, or set up cones to mark the perimeter of the goal. You have the option of using a goalkeeper during this drill or keeping an open net. Split your team into two lines.

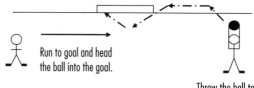

Run to goal and head the ball into the goal.

Throw the ball to the center of the goal.

Figure 11.4

Side Heading

Player needs: Put all of the soccer balls with the group of players throwing the balls.

Drill execution: Place one group of players on one side of the goal and the other group on the opposite side of the goal. The groups should be facing each other. The group doing the throwing has all of the balls. The thrower will be about 10 steps from the goalpost and about 5 steps off of the end line. The player heading the ball starts approximately 15 steps beyond the goalpost on his or her side and lines up even with the player throwing the ball.

The player who is heading the ball takes off, and at the same time the player throwing the ball places it to the runner. The runner continues to the ball and then heads the ball left or right into the goal. Have all of the players head the ball to their left a few times and then rotate and repeat the drill while heading the ball to the right.

Coaching Tips

1. Make sure the player running toward the thrower watches the player throwing the ball and adjusts to center on the ball when the ball is thrown.

2. Ensure the player throwing in the ball places the ball in line and in front of the approaching player and at the correct distance. Accuracy of the throw-in is a must.

3. Watch to ensure the player heading the ball moves to the ball and then uses proper heading techniques to place the ball to the left or right and into the goal.

Throw and Shoot   (Figure 11.5)

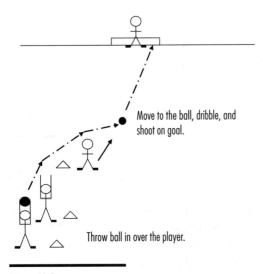

Move to the ball, dribble, and shoot on goal.

Throw ball in over the player.

Figure 11.5
Throw and Shoot

Purpose: The distance of a throw-in is as important as accuracy. This drill teaches the players to throw the ball high and far.

Preparation: Use a goal, or set up cones to mark the perimeter of the goal. Players will be in a line, and three players will be used for each repetition of the drill. Use three cones to mark where the players stand. Place your goalkeeper in the goal.

Player needs: The player doing the throw-in needs to have a ball.

Drill execution: Put three players in a straight line. The first in line is the player throwing the ball. The next player will be two or three steps from the player throwing the ball and will be facing the thrower. This player stands still with hands in the air. This requires the player doing the throw-in to throw the ball into the air high enough to clear the player in front. Players cannot put their hands in the air during a game but can for the purpose of this drill. Make sure they know this so they don't get a penalty during the game. The player receiving the ball will be 10 steps from the second player and facing the goal but with head turned to watch the throw-in.

The player doing the throw-in throws the ball over the outreached hands of the player in front. As the ball is thrown, the player receiving the ball moves to the ball and controls it. Once that player has control of the ball, he or she dribbles to the goal and shoots, making sure the shot is away from the goalkeeper. The drill can also be done by throwing the ball over the players so the player shooting has to turn, go to the ball, and shoot.

Coaching Tips

1. Watch the players doing the throw-ins to ensure they keep their hands even on the ball and do not lift their feet off of the ground.

2. Check to see that the ball goes into the air in an arc and is near the player receiving the ball.

3. Be sure that when the ball is thrown, the player receiving it moves instantly to adjust to the placement of the ball.

4. Make sure the player who receives the ball gains control and then moves directly to the goal. The shot on goal should be away from the goalkeeper.

Throw, Head, and Shoot (Figure 11.6)

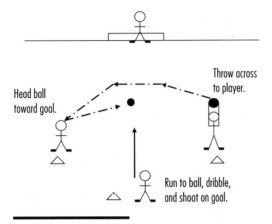

Throw across to player.

Head ball toward goal.

Run to ball, dribble, and shoot on goal.

Figure 11.6
Throw, Head, and Shoot

Purpose: The ability to throw, head, and shoot is very valuable. This drill lets the players get creative on all of these techniques.

Preparation: Use a goal, or set up cones to mark the perimeter of the goal. Set up three cones to form a triangle with approximately 10 steps between each cone. Split your team into three groups with each group behind a cone. Place your goalkeeper in the goal.

Player needs: One ball is needed for every three players.

Drill execution: Place the player throwing the ball to one side. Place the player heading the ball opposite to and facing that player. The third player is between the two players but back from them and away from the goal.

The player who is doing the throw-in will throw the ball across to the player who heads the ball. As soon as the ball is thrown, the player in the middle, who is the shooter, starts moving straight down the field. The player heading the ball heads it toward the goal so the player running past can gain control, dribble to the goal, and shoot. After each repetition of the drill, make sure players switch places. Make sure your goalkeeper plays the ball and moves to reduce the angle of the shot on goal.

Coaching Tips

1. Make sure the throw-in is in the air for a proper heading and that it has the proper distance and accuracy.

2. Watch to see if the player heading the ball adjusts to the position of the ball and uses proper heading techniques.

3. Ensure the shooter moves as soon as the ball is thrown. That player should watch the ball to gauge where the ball is going to be placed.

4. Make sure that as soon as the ball is headed, the shooter moves to the ball, gains control, dribbles to the goal, and shoots.

5. Check that the shot is away from the goalkeeper.

Turn and Shoot   (Figure 11.7)

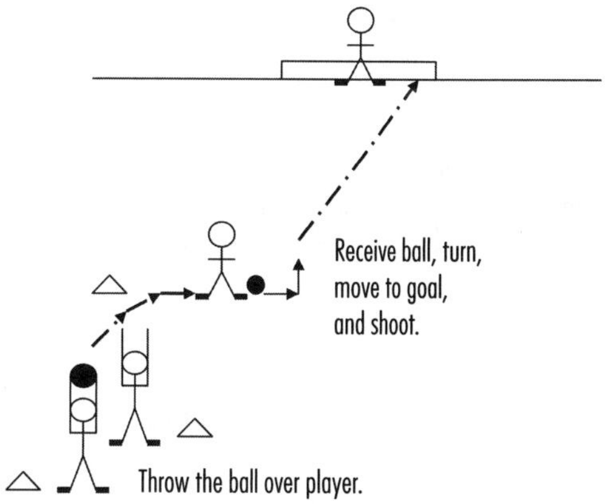

Purpose: This drill uses the throw-in, heading, and different techniques for receiving the ball. It also incorporates dribbling and shooting.

Preparation: Use a goal, or set up cones to mark the perimeter of the goal. Use three cones to mark the placement of the three players. Place the first two cones three steps apart and the third cone five or more steps from the second cone. Use three players for each drill, and make multiple lines of three. Use your goalkeeper by putting him or her in the goal.

Player needs: Each group of three needs one ball.

Drill execution: Have the players stand beside the cones. The player throwing the ball throws over the player with the outstretched arms to a player behind that middle player. The player doing the throw-in and the player standing in the middle will be facing each other. The player receiving the ball will be facing the player doing the throw-in.

Receive ball, turn, move to goal, and shoot.

Throw the ball over player.

Figure 11.7
Turn and Shoot

   The player receiving the ball uses the proper technique to capture the ball with head, chest, thighs, or feet. The player can use whatever technique is the best to receive and control the ball. After gaining control, the player turns, dribbles to the goal, and shoots. Have the goalkeeper watch the ball and move to reduce the angle of the shot.

Coaching Tips

1. Watch the throw-in to check that the player uses proper throwing techniques and does not lift the feet off of the ground.

2. Make sure the player receiving the ball uses the proper technique to capture and control the ball.

3. Ensure the player with the ball makes a proper turn and dribbles with control to the goal.

4. Be sure the shot on goal is accurate and away from the goalkeeper.

Throw-In and Shoot   (Figure 11.8)

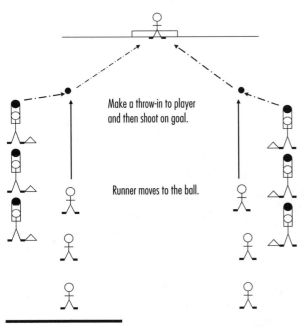

Make a throw-in to player and then shoot on goal.

Runner moves to the ball.

Figure 11.8
Throw-In and Shoot

Purpose: This drill trains players to gauge the proper placement for a throw-in. It trains the player doing the throw-in and the player receiving the ball.

Preparation: Use a goal, or set up cones to mark the perimeter of the goal. Split your team into groups of two. Place cones along the touchline. You will need one cone for each player doing the throw-in. Line up the players receiving the ball so they are running straight down the touchline but approximately five steps away from the player doing the throw-in. Place your goal-keeper in the goal.

Player needs: Each team of two players needs one ball.

Drill execution: The player doing the throw-in slaps a hand on the side of the ball to indicate when the runner is to take off. The throw will be made so it is in front of the running player. The throw needs to be in the direction of the goal area and with proper distance. The player will run to the ball or if close enough will receive the ball, control it, and dribble to the goal and shoot. Change the two players after each drill set.

Start the drill at the end closest to the goal. As the throw-in is made, the next player in line does a throw-in. This keeps the drill moving and does not have players interfering with the play of the rest of the team. Have your goalkeeper move so he or she is in a position to stop the ball before it enters the goal.

Coaching Tips

1. Make sure the throw-in is done properly. The throw should be made with the proper accuracy and distance. The thrower's feet should not leave the ground during the throw-in.

2. When the player doing the throw-in slaps the side of the ball, make sure the runner takes off and moves down the field and in front of the player doing the throw-in.

3. When the ball is thrown, check to see the player receiving the ball moves to the ball, captures it, controls it, and then dribbles to the goal and shoots.

4. Be sure the shot on goal is quick and away from the goalkeeper.

Passing and Shooting Drills

There are relatively few game situations where a goal is scored without passing being involved. When a pass to another player results in a score, this is called an assist. All assists happen because the team with the ball has been able to move the ball to create a situation where a goal can be scored. The following combination drills are designed to move the ball down the field, with the team finishing by scoring a goal.

Triangle Pass and Shoot   (Figure 11.9)

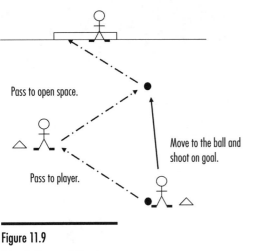

Pass to open space.

Pass to player.

Move to the ball and shoot on goal.

Figure 11.9
Triangle Pass and Shoot

Purpose: This drill is a combination of passing the ball one direction and having it returned in the opposite direction so the shooter is now in a better position to shoot on goal.

Preparation: Use a goal, or set up cones to mark the perimeter of the goal. You will also need two cones to mark the area for the start of the drill. One cone will be placed approximately at the edge of the penalty box. This cone is for the shooter. The second cone is at a 45-degree angle to the left or right and approximately 10 steps in front of the back cone. Two players plus the goalkeeper participate in this drill. Multiple players can be set up across the front of the goal to do this drill. After completion of each repetition of this drill, the two players change positions.

Player needs: One ball is needed for each set of two players.

Drill execution: The first player, the one farthest from the goal, passes the ball to the other player. As soon as this player passes the ball, he or she runs toward the goal. The player receiving the ball then passes the ball to open space in front of the goal. The shooter moves to the ball and shoots on goal.

Coaching Tips

1. Make sure the initial pass is accurate.

2. Watch the player receiving the initial pass to make sure that player controls the ball. The next pass is to open space in front of the shooter. The pass should not be to the shooter but to open space in front of the shooter.

3. Ensure the shooter goes to the ball, centers on it, and shoots quickly and accurately.

Trail and Shoot (Figure 11.10)

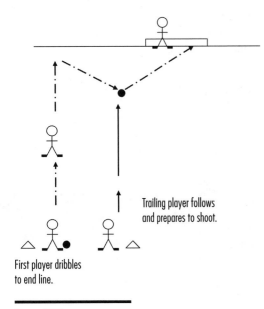

Trailing player follows
and prepares to shoot.

First player dribbles
to end line.

Figure 11.10

Trail and Shoot

Purpose: This drill teaches players how to move the ball and to shadow the player with the ball to get a shooting opportunity.

Preparation: Use a goal, or set up cones to mark the perimeter of the goal. Teams are split into two, and two cones are needed to mark their positions. These cones are approximately 20 steps from the goal and are spaced 10 steps apart. Cones can be set on each side of the field.

Player needs: Each team of two players needs one ball.

Drill execution: Place the two players beside their cones. The player on the outside starts dribbling toward the end line. After that player has moved approximately five steps, the second player takes off and runs straight down the field toward the end line and maintaining the five-step distance behind the player with the ball.

When the player with the ball gets to the end line, that player passes the ball so it goes in front of the trailing player. That player then shoots on goal.

Coaching Tips

1. Watch the player with the ball to ensure he or she dribbles down the field properly and with speed.

2. Ensure the trailing player starts after the first player has moved approximately five steps down the field.

3. Check to see that the trailing player maintains both the distance behind the lead player and separation from the lead player.

4. Watch that the pass is in front of the trailing player.

5. Ensure the shooter moves to the ball and shoots quickly and accurately.

Pass and Move   (Figure 11.11)

Purpose: This drill teaches passing, moving to open space, centering the ball, moving down the field, and shooting on goal. This drill covers everything that is necessary to properly perform in a game.

Preparation: Use a goal, or set up cones to mark the perimeter of the goal. Place three cones on the center line. The first cone is just a few feet outside of the touchline although the player will be standing inside the touchline even with the cone. This keeps the cone from interfering with the passing of the ball. The second cone is approximately 10 large steps from the first cone. The third cone is aligned with the left post, or far post of the goal. Each drill requires three players.

Player needs: Each team of three players needs one ball.

Drill execution: This drill is started by the player in the center, who passes the ball to the player near the touchline. After the pass, the player that passed the ball moves toward the corner flag. The player near the touchline receives the ball and passes the ball down the touchline toward the

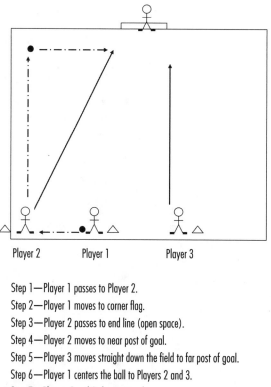

Player 2   Player 1   Player 3

Step 1—Player 1 passes to Player 2.
Step 2—Player 1 moves to corner flag.
Step 3—Player 2 passes to end line (open space).
Step 4—Player 2 moves to near post of goal.
Step 5—Player 3 moves straight down the field to far post of goal.
Step 6—Player 1 centers the ball to Players 2 and 3.
Step 7—Players 2 and 3 shoot on goal.

Figure 11.11
Pass and Move

end line. This pass is into open space. As the player near the touchline passes the ball, that player moves down the field and goes straight to the near post. The third player moves down the field, staying in line with the ball, and moves to the rear post of the goal. The player who made the first pass catches up with the ball, moves to near the end line, and then centers the ball to the two players near the goal. One of these players shoots on goal. Have players switch lines with each repetition of the drill.

To get more players involved, set up this drill so it can be run from the right side of the field and then the left side of the field. Keep the drill moving at a fast pace.

Coaching Tips

1. Do not let players hesitate before they pass. All passes should be done properly. A quick and accurate pass is a must.

2. Make sure your players move after passing the ball.

3. Watch your players to ensure they do not move into an offside position. The two players off the ball should maintain their positions relative to the ball and not advance to a position in front of the ball.

4. When the two players are near the goal, make sure the player on the near post is in front of the goalkeeper and the player on the far post is away from the goal to get any ball that is centered wide of the goal.

5. Confirm that the centering of the ball is into the goal area but to a player and away from the goalkeeper.

Flick and Move   (Figure 11.12)

Purpose: This drill teaches ball control, passing, and shooting on goal. It is not a move used on the field that often, but it is helpful to develop touch on the ball and the ability to shoot on goal.

Preparation: Use a goal, or set up cones to mark the perimeter of the goal. Split your team in two. One player is used to pass the ball, and one player is used to flick the ball over the head and move to the goal and shoot. Place cones across the field to mark where the person passing the ball starts. Use as many cones as you need to place all of your players in teams across the field. The cones should be approximately 20 steps from the goal.

Player needs: Each team of two players needs one ball.

Drill execution: The player with the ball starts the drill by passing the ball to the player up the field and facing them. The player receiving the ball moves to the ball, lets it roll up the foot, and flicks it backward over the head. That player then turns and moves to the ball. Once the player reaches the ball, that player dribbles to the goal and shoots around the goalkeeper. Players switch positions with each repetition of the drill.

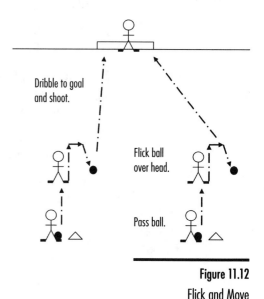

Dribble to goal and shoot.

Flick ball over head.

Pass ball.

Figure 11.12

Flick and Move

Coaching Tips

1. Make sure the pass is to the player and has enough speed to allow the player receiving the ball to flick the ball.

2. Be sure the player receiving the ball moves to center on the ball and places a foot in the path of the ball.

3. Watch the player receiving the ball to ensure that player lifts the foot to flick the ball over the head. That player will have to lean back slightly to make this flick.

4. After the ball goes over the head of the player, make sure the player turns and goes directly to the ball.

5. Watch that the dribble is controlled and that the shot on goal is accurate and away from the goalkeeper.

Drop and Shoot (Figure 11.13)

Purpose: This drill teaches players to be aware of where they are on the field. It also requires communication among players. It is a timing drill that uses passing, dribbling, and shooting.

Preparation: Use a goal, or set up cones to mark the perimeter of the goal. Set cones as the starting point, and place these cones approximately 20 steps away from the goal. Split the team into two players each. Rotate players after each repetition of the drill.

Player needs: Each team of two players needs one ball.

Drill execution: Line up the players one behind the other and approximately five steps from each other. Both players will be facing the goal. The first player in line, the one closest to the goal, has the ball. The drill is started with the front player dribbling straight down the field. The second

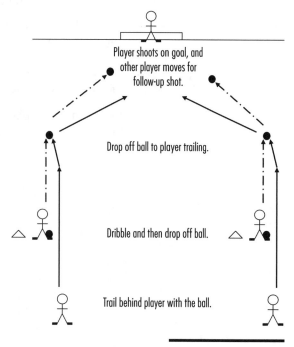

Figure 11.13
Drop and Shoot

player follows staying approximately five steps back from the front player. When the lead player dribbles halfway to the goal, that player drops off the ball and moves to the right or left to center on the goal.

The second player, the one trailing the first, picks up the ball on the run, dribbles to the goal, and shoots. The first player is in position to take any secondary shot.

Coaching Tips

1. Make sure the player that is trailing keeps his or her distance from the player dribbling and moves in unison with the front player.

2. When the ball is dropped off, make sure the second player quickly advances to the ball.

3. Make sure the player that drops the ball goes lateral staying even with the ball so he or she is not in an offside situation.

4. Watch that both players advance to the goal after the shot. It is important that both players move into position to get a secondary shot if possible.

Volley Drills

Self Half Volley Shot   (Figure 11.14)

Purpose: This drill allows players to shoot while the ball is in the air but on a bounce. Shooting fast without settling the ball gives the shooter an advantage.

Preparation: Use a goal, or set up cones to mark the perimeter of the goal. Have each player line up on the penalty box line. If no line is present, mark the line with cones to let the players know where to stand.

Player needs: Each player will need a ball.

Drill execution: Start with a player on either the far right or left side of the line, and move straight down the line letting each player do the drill. To start this drill, have the first player throw the ball into the air and then move to the ball. After the ball has hit the ground, bounced back into the air, and is dropping back down, have the player strike the ball while it is still in the air. The shot should go directly to the goal. As soon as the ball has been shot on goal and played by the goalkeeper, move to the next player in line.

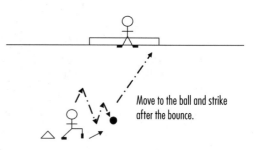

Move to the ball and strike after the bounce.

Figure 11.14
Self Half Volley Shot

Coaching Tips

1. Make sure the player with the ball throws the ball high into the air to get the ball to bounce. The ball should also be in front of the player.

2. Watch to ensure the player quickly moves to the ball and centers on the ball.

3. Check that after the ball has hit the ground and bounces back up the player is in the right position. As the ball starts back down, the player should have a knee in the air, leg down and back, toe pointed toward the ground, and ankle locked. That player then swings a foot through the ball, striking it with the laces of the shoe.

4. Be sure that after striking the ball, the player moves in the direction of the kick to get a follow-up shot if possible.

Throw Half Volley Shot   (Figure 11.15)

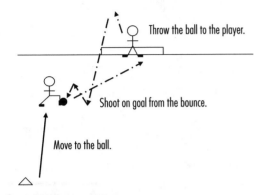

Throw the ball to the player.

Shoot on goal from the bounce.

Move to the ball.

Figure 11.15
Throw Half Volley Shot

Purpose: This drill allows players to move to the ball and shoot while the ball is in the air but on a bounce. Shooting fast without settling the ball gives the shooter an advantage.

Preparation: Use a goal, or set up cones to mark the perimeter of the goal. Have each player line up on the penalty box line. If no line is present, mark the line with cones to let the players know where to stand.

Player needs: Each player needs a ball.

Drill execution: Start with a player on either the far right or left side of the line and move straight down the line, letting each player do the drill. The first player passes the ball to the goalkeeper. The goalkeeper then throws the ball into the air toward the player that passed the ball. That player moves to the ball and centers on the ball. After the ball has hit the ground and bounces back into the air, the player strikes the ball while it is still in the air but is on the downward drop. The shot should go directly to the goal. As soon as the ball has been shot on goal and played by the goalkeeper, move to the next player in line.

Coaching Tips

1. Make sure the pass to the goalkeeper is strong and accurate. The goal-keeper should not have to run to get the ball.

2. Have the goalkeeper throw the ball high into the air to get the ball to bounce. The ball should also be in front of the player.

3. Watch to ensure the player quickly moves to the ball and centers on the ball.

4. Check to see that after the ball has hit the ground and bounced back up, the player is in position. As the ball starts back down, the player should have a knee in the air, leg down and back, toe pointing toward the ground, and ankle locked. That player then swings the foot through the ball, striking it with the laces of the shoe.

5. Watch that the player, after striking the ball, moves in the direction of the kick to get a follow-up shot if possible.

Self Full Volley Shot   (Figure 11.16)

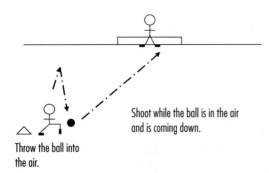

Shoot while the ball is in the air
and is coming down.

Throw the ball into
the air.

Figure 11.16
Self Full Volley Shot

Purpose: This drill teaches players to move to the ball and shoot while the ball is still in the air. Shooting fast without settling the ball gives the shooter an advantage.

Preparation: Use a goal, or set up cones to mark the perimeter of the goal. Have each player line up on the penalty box line. If no line is present, mark the line with cones to let the players know where to stand.

Player needs: Each player needs a ball.

Drill execution: Start with a player on either the far right or left side of the line, and move straight down the line until each player does the drill. Have the first player throw the ball high into the air. The ball should be almost straight up and close to the player. That player moves to the ball and centers on it. While the ball is coming down but still in the air, the player strikes the ball. The ball must be kicked on the downward drop. The shot should go directly to the goal. As soon as the ball has been shot on goal and played by the goalkeeper, move to the next player in line.

Coaching Tips

1. Make sure the player throws the ball high into the air, but near enough so there is less space to cover. The ball should also be in front of the player.

2. Watch to ensure the player quickly moves to the ball and centers on the ball.

3. Be sure that as the ball is coming down, the player moves into position in front of the ball. As the ball starts back down, the player should have a knee in the air, leg down and back, toe pointing toward the ground, and ankle locked. The player then swings the foot through the ball, striking it with the laces of the shoe.

4. Watch that after striking the ball, the player moves in the direction of the kick to get a follow-up shot if possible.

Throw Full Volley Shot   (Figure 11.17)

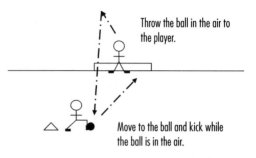

Purpose: This drill helps players move to the ball and shoot while the ball is still in the air and has not touched the ground. Shooting fast without settling the ball gives the shooter an advantage.

Throw the ball in the air to the player.

Move to the ball and kick while the ball is in the air.

Figure 11.17
Throw Full Volley Shot

Preparation: Use a goal, or set up cones to mark the perimeter of the goal. Have each player lined up about 10 steps out from the goalkeeper. Place a cone to mark where the players stand to do this drill.

Player needs: Each player needs a ball.

Drill execution: Start with a player on either the far right or left side of the line and move straight down the line, letting each player do the drill. Have the first player pass the ball directly to the goalkeeper. The goalkeeper scoops up the ball and then throws it, underhanded, into the air toward the player who passed the ball. The ball should be high and close to the player. That player moves to the ball and centers on the ball. While the ball is in the air, the player strikes the ball. The ball should be on the downward drop, and the shot should go directly to the goal. As soon as the ball has been shot on goal and played by the goalkeeper, move to the next player in line.

Coaching Tips

1. Check that the pass to the goalkeeper is direct and with enough force to allow the goalkeeper to play the ball. The pass should be directly to the goalkeeper so the goalkeeper does not have to chase the ball.

2. Make sure the goalkeeper throws the ball high into the air but near the player so the player can easily move to the ball. The ball should also be in front of the player.

3. Watch to ensure the player quickly moves to the ball and centers on the ball.

4. See whether as the ball is coming down the player moves into position in front of the ball. As the ball starts back down, the player should have the knee in the air, leg down and back, toe pointing toward the ground, and ankle locked. The player then swings the foot through the ball, striking it with the laces of the shoe.

5. Ensure that after striking the ball, the player moves in the direction of the kick to get a follow-up shot if possible.

CHAPTER 12

Offense and Defense Drills

Using drills that improve offensive and defensive skills is a must. Players need to be able to do drills that allow them to develop the technique without opposition, but once they have mastered the skill then it is time to place the players into actual game situations. These game situations are crucial to creating a team that is competitive. Learning soccer is done in steps. You start with the basics and then move forward until your players all move as one and execute plays that result in overcoming the other team's defense with a score.

The drills in this chapter are designed to prepare your players to know what to do while on the field in actual game situations. These drills incorporate the techniques learned elsewhere in this book. All of these drills, as well as most of the others in this book, require a goalkeeper. Training the goalkeeper on what to do along with the rest of the team is also a must.

NOTE: In all of these drills, when the defense captures the ball they do not kick the ball down the field. They must dribble and pass to get back to the center line. Or you can place cones to the outside of the field on each side, and when the defense gets the ball, they pass to that cone. Kicking the ball hard down the field is a waste of time. Make sure the players use skills they will use during a game.

Drills

Back and Forth to the Goal   (Figure 12.1)

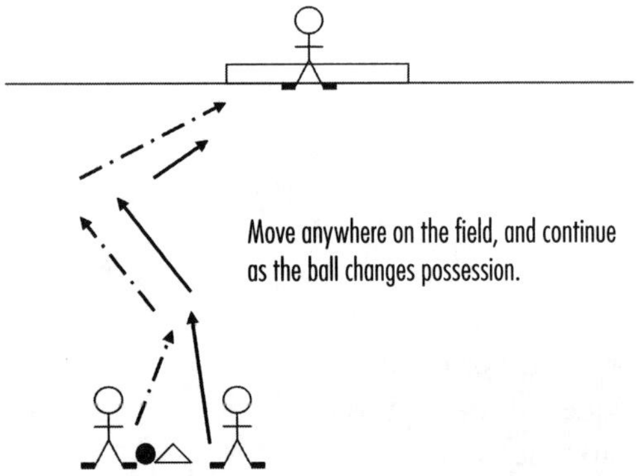

Move anywhere on the field, and continue as the ball changes possession.

Figure 12.1
Back and Forth
to the Goal

Purpose: This drill places each player in a situation to play offense and defense.

Preparation: Use a goal, or mark the perimeter of the goal using cones. Divide your players into units of twos. Try to match players who have about the same abilities. The players will be on the center line of the field. If you do not have field markings, use cones to mark the center line.

Player needs: Each team of two players needs one ball.

Drill execution: Start play by blowing your whistle. The player with the ball dribbles toward the goal. That player is the offensive player. The other player takes off and tries to capture the ball. That player is the defense. If the defensive player captures the ball from the offensive player, that player now becomes the offensive player and moves on the goal. The player who lost the ball now becomes the defensive player. The ball can switch numerous times before one of the players actually gets a shot on goal. When this team has shot on goal, have the players move to the outside of the field and return to the center line. After the shot, start the next team.

Coaching Tips

1. Match players who have skills that are similar. You want each team to be competitive.

2. Emphasize moving to open space for the offensive player. Make sure you stress the principle of immediate chase to the defensive player. The player must get the ball or put pressure on the player with the ball.

3. Watch for proper dribbling techniques. Let the players use their imaginations and make any moves necessary to maintain control and then get open for a shot on goal.

4. Watch to see that the ball changes between the two players if proper defense is being used.

5. Make sure the shot on goal is taken when the player has an opening. Players should shoot fast, hard, and accurately.

Two on One (Figure 12.2)

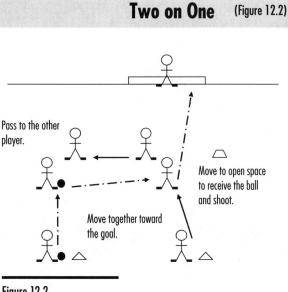

Pass to the other player.

Move to open space to receive the ball and shoot.

Move together toward the goal.

Figure 12.2
Two on One

Purpose: This drill teaches players how to get the defense to commit, when to pass, and how to move to open space.

Preparation: Use a goal, or use cones to mark the perimeter of the goal. Split your team into two players for offense and one player for defense. The two players on offense need one ball. Using cones, mark the starting point that is near midfield. The offensive players should be approximately 10 steps apart to start the drill. The defensive player will be on the penalty box line. Mark this area with a cone.

Player needs: The two offensive players need one ball.

Drill execution: Blow your whistle to start the drill. One player starts dribbling toward the goal. The second player moves with and stays even with that player. The player dribbling must make the defensive player commit to him or her. The player with the ball can go anywhere and must pull the defensive player to him or her. The defensive player must move to the player with the ball but must also know where the second player is on the field. Once the defensive player has committed and is approximately two steps from the offensive players, the player dribbling passes the ball to the other offensive player. The second player must move to a position that is open in order to receive the pass. That player either shoots on goal or, if the defensive player is able to get there before a shot is taken, that offensive player passes back to the partner.

Rotate your players so all play offense and defense.

Coaching Tips

1. Watch that the players dribble as if in a game; they cannot just walk down the field.

2. Make sure the player with the ball pulls the defensive player to defend them. This opens the second offensive player.

3. Make sure the second offensive player is not too close to the player with the ball. If the second player is too close to the other offensive player, the defensive player will be able to get to that player after the pass. But the second player must not be so far away that he or she cannot receive the ball.

4. Tell players that when they receive the ball, they must shoot on goal if they are open. They cannot delay the kick to get into what they think is a better position. A quick shot is best.

Two on Two   (Figure 12.3)

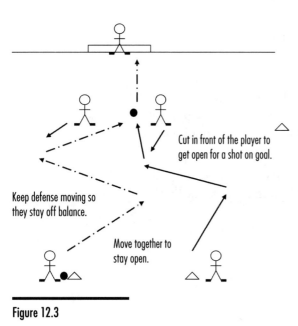

Cut in front of the player to
get open for a shot on goal.

Keep defense moving so
they stay off balance.

Move together to
stay open.

Figure 12.3
Two on Two

Purpose: This drill teaches the offense and defense to play as a team. It also requires the offensive players to move to keep the defense in a moving or chase position.

Preparation: Use a goal, or use cones to mark the perimeter of the goal. Pick two players to play defense and two players to play offense. Rotate after each drill. Place the two offensive players near midfield, and mark their positions with cones. They should be approximately 10 steps apart. The two defensive players should be at the edge of the penalty box. Mark their positions by using a cone outside the area of play.

Player needs: The two offensive players need one ball.

Drill execution: Blow your whistle to start play. The offensive players can go anywhere on the field. The player without the ball must move to stay open to receive the pass. This player can overlap or move in any direction. The defensive players must stay in their positions to force the player with the ball to the outside of the goal and keep the other player from getting into a position to receive the ball and shoot on goal. The defensive player on the player with the ball must move to that player to either capture the ball or force a pass. The second defender must be in a position to cut off the pass to the second offensive player. If the player with the ball moves from one side of the field to the other, make sure the defense uses good communication so no offensive player gets open.

Coaching Tips

1. Make sure the player with the ball uses proper dribbling techniques. That player can dribble anywhere on the field and does not have to go straight down the field. The dribbler can go across the face of the goal, go back, or go anywhere else.

2. Be sure the second player does not move to an offside position. The second player must constantly adjust to the player with the ball so he or she can stay open to receive a pass.

3. Watch the second offensive player to make sure that player is constantly moving to stay in an open position. Communication between the offensive players is a must. If the second player cuts between the two defensive players, that second player must let the player with the ball know what he or she is doing.

4. Watch to see that the player with the ball dribbles with the head up and passes before being cornered by the defense. If that player is forced to shield the ball, the second offensive player must move quickly to get in an open position to receive the ball.

5. Encourage either offensive player to shoot quickly when open with the ball.

6. Ensure your defensive players stay in their primary and support positions to capture the ball during a pass or a center.

Three on Three (Figure 12.4)

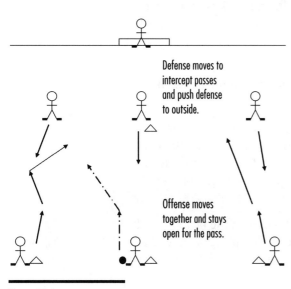

Defense moves to intercept passes and push defense to outside.

Offense moves together and stays open for the pass.

Figure 12.4
Three on Three

Purpose: This drill is as close to real game conditions as you can get. It requires the defensive players to work together and the offensive players to work together.

Preparation: Use a goal, or set up cones to mark the perimeter of the goal. Place three cones near the center of the field to mark the starting point for the offense. Place a saucer cone near the penalty box line for the defense. Place three players inside the penalty box as the defense. Place three offensive players near the cones at midfield.

Player needs: The three offensive players need one ball.

Drill execution: To start the drill, blow your whistle. The defenders cannot move beyond their cone until you have started play by blowing the whistle. The offense moves the ball toward the goal, working as a team. If players are out of position, blow the whistle twice to stop play and freeze the players where they are. Do not let them move after play stops. After the drill is run, the offensive players move to defense and the defensive players go to midfield and become the offense. Repeat the drill with these new positions.

Coaching Tips

1. Watch that your offensive players move the ball using proper dribbling and passing techniques. They must move with their heads up.

2. Remind the player with the ball not to pass until challenged or until there is an opportunity because a defensive player is out of position.

3. Check that the two offensive players off the ball are always in a position where they can see the ball and the player with the ball can see their full bodies. They must stay on the ball side of the defensive players.

4. Make sure the offense moves in different directions and does not just go straight down the field. The offense must get the defense moving to take away the defensive advantage.

5. See that the defense is constantly moving in order to shut down opportunities for passes by the offense.

6. Stop play and tell the players to freeze if mistakes are made, i.e., players are behind other players, the passing is poor, and so on. Walk players through the mistakes they are making, and then restart play or repeat with the same group.

Throw and Move   (Figure 12.5)

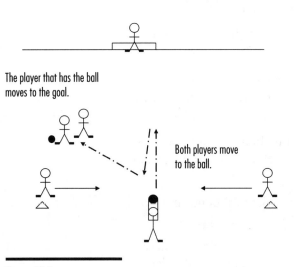

The player that has the ball moves to the goal.

Both players move to the ball.

Figure 12.5
Throw and Move

Purpose: A good aggression development drill, this drill pits one player against another. Play starts when a player wins the ball, and each player can switch from offense to defense.

Preparation: Use a goal, or use cones to mark the perimeter of the goal. Place two cones approximately 20 steps apart near midfield. Split the team into two groups, with one group near one cone and the other group near the other cone.

Player needs: Players do not need any equipment; the balls are with the coach.

Drill execution: With your players near the cones and on separate sides of the field, throw the ball high into the air. As soon as the ball is thrown, the first player on each side moves to the ball. The player that captures the ball becomes the offense and tries to move to the goal. The other player is the defense and tries to take the ball away. If the ball changes players, the one with the ball is the offense. Players move to the goal, and the player who gets open shoots on goal.

Coaching Tips

1. Make sure that both players go directly to the ball when it is in the air.

2. Observe the techniques the players use to capture the ball.

3. When one player has captured the ball, make sure this player moves away from the opponent to open space and makes the defensive player chase.

4. Watch for proper shielding, cuts, and moves by the offensive player.

5. Watch the defensive player for proper actions to move to the outside of the field and/or capture the ball. The defensive player should stay goal side or between the player with the ball and the goal.

6. Watch that the shot on goal is taken when the first opportunity arises and that shots are not passed up.

Throw and Turn   (Figure 12.6)

Purpose: This drill teaches the defense how to move to and turn the ball. It teaches the offense how to capture the ball before the defense can turn it.

Preparation: Use a goal or cones to mark the perimeter of the goal. Split the team into groups of two. One will be the offense and the other the defense. Players change positions with each repetition of the drill. Place as many cones as you need across the field near midfield to mark the starting point of the drill. Place one row for the defense and one row about 10 steps back for the offense. By using multiple cones you can include all of you players and not have them standing around and waiting.

Player needs: Each team of two players needs one ball.

Drill execution: The player in the rear, the offensive player, does a throw-in over the head of the defensive player. The defensive player moves to the ball and tries to turn it and bring it back to the starting point. The offensive player tries to capture the ball before the defensive player can turn the ball. If the offensive player cannot capture the ball before the turn, that player must give immediate chase to apply pressure and gain possession of the ball.

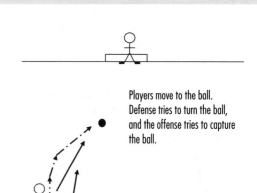

Players move to the ball. Defense tries to turn the ball, and the offense tries to capture the ball.

Figure 12.6

Throw and Turn

Coaching Tips

1. Make sure the throw-in is done properly and that both of the player's feet remain on the ground. The throw should be high to go over the head of the defense and as far down the field as possible.

2. Check that the defensive player immediately takes off after the ball and the offensive player follows the defensive player to the ball.

3. Watch to ensure the defensive player gains control of the ball and moves to the outside to dribble or pass the ball.

4. Watch to see if the offensive player moves to take the ball away before or on the turn.

Chip and Turn   (Figure 12.7)

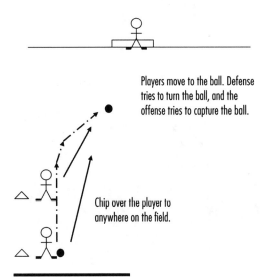

Players move to the ball. Defense tries to turn the ball, and the offense tries to capture the ball.

Chip over the player to anywhere on the field.

Figure 12.7
Chip and Turn

Purpose: This drill is similar to the previous drill but uses a chip to get the ball down the field rather than a throw-in. It is a one-on-one situation in which the defense tries to get to the ball and turn it while the offense tries to capture the ball on the turn.

Preparation: Use a goal or cones to mark the perimeter of the goal. Split the team into groups of two. One will be offense and the other defense. Players change positions with each repetition of the drill. Place as many cones as you need across the field near midfield to mark the starting point of the drill. Place one row for the defense and one row about 15 steps back for the offense. By using multiple cones placed across the field you can include all of your players and not have them standing around and waiting.

Player needs: Each team of two players needs one ball.

Drill execution: The player in the rear, the offensive player, chips the ball over the head of the defensive player. The chip can be to any point on the field. Moving to the ball, the defensive player tries to turn it and bring it back or pass it back to the starting point. The pass should be to either one of the starting cones. This allows them a choice and also gives them a chance to work on their accuracy. The offensive player tries to capture the ball before the defensive player can turn the ball. If the offensive player cannot capture the ball before the turn, that player must give immediate chase to apply pressure or gain possession.

Coaching Tips

1. Make sure the chip is in the air and clears the defensive player. The chip should be high to go over the head of the defense and as far down the field as possible.

2. Check to see that the defensive player immediately takes off after the ball and the offensive player follows the defensive player to the ball.

3. Watch to ensure the defensive player gains control of the ball and moves to the outside to dribble or pass the ball.

4. Watch the offensive player to see if that player moves to take the ball away before or on the turn.

Through the Box (Figure 12.8)

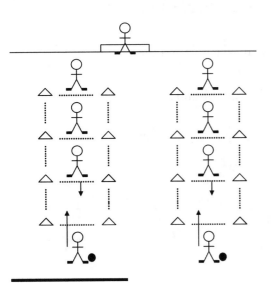

Figure 12.8
Through the Box

Purpose: This drill requires a player to go through several levels of defense before shooting on goal.

Preparation: Use a goal, or mark the perimeter of the goal using cones. Lay out boxes using cones. Start with one box, and then add a second and then a third as the player's proficiency increases. The boxes should be at least 10 steps square.

Player needs: Each offensive player needs a ball.

Drill execution: Place one player at the back of the box. This player is the defense and is closest to the goal. As the offensive player dribbles into the square the defensive player can move forward. The defense must stay at the back of the box until the offensive player enters the box. Neither player can move outside the box. The player with the ball tries to get past the defensive player and shoot. This requires the player to maneuver in a small area to get past the defense to shoot on goal. Switch players from offense to defense after each repetition of the drill. This is a difficult drill, and few players will make it through the box when you first start. However, your players will improve the more you do the drill. They will learn to operate in small areas.

As your players become more proficient, add an additional box with another defender. Keep this going until you have three boxes, three defenders, and one offensive player.

Coaching Tips

1. Watch the player with the ball to ensure he or she properly protects the ball.

2. Ensure that your defensive player stays at the back line until the player with the ball enters the marked play area.

3. Encourage your offensive players to be creative to gain the advantage and move the ball past the defensive player.

4. Do not let the defensive player use his or her hands to push or hold the offensive player.

Center and Shoot (Figure 12.9)

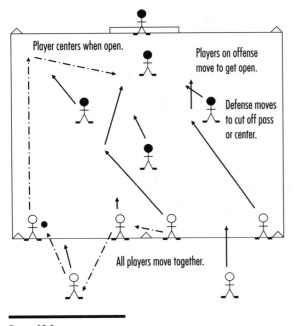

Player centers when open.

Players on offense move to get open.

Defense moves to cut off pass or center.

All players move together.

Figure 12.9
Center and Shoot

Purpose: This drill teaches your team how to center the ball in front of the goal to increase your scoring opportunities. The drill is demonstrated with four fullbacks and three forwards and three halfbacks but can be done with whatever formation you choose. The same principles apply. The purpose is to spread out the defense to create openings.

Preparation: Use a goal, or use cones to mark the perimeter of the goal. Place cones to mark the corner flags. Place cones on the center line as a starting point for the drill.

Player needs: The offensive players need one ball.

Drill execution: Start play by using a kickoff. Pass the ball back to the halfback to give the forwards time to move down the field. The halfback will move the ball down the outside of the field and pass to the forward when that person is open. This forward with the ball will take the ball down the field to the end line. That player will then kick the ball to center it and get it in front of the goal. As the player with the ball has been moving down the field, the remaining forwards stay even with the ball so they are not offside. The halfbacks move down the field behind their perspective forward to maintain support and separation. When the ball is centered the other offensive players move to the ball and quickly shoot on goal. It is essential to move the ball to the outside of the field and take the ball as close as the player can to the end line. The defensive players must maintain their formation so there are no openings to the goal. If the ball is centered, the defensive players need to get to the ball and get it out of the goal area as fast as they can.

Coaching Tips

1. Use whatever kickoff formation you normally use. Watch that the players do this properly.

2. Observe your players to make sure they use proper passing techniques to move the ball down the field.

3. Be sure the ball goes to a forward on the outside of the field. This player will move the ball to the end line and cross the ball to the center of the field. Watch that the ball goes into the goal front area but is out and away from the goalkeeper.

4. Watch that when the ball enters the goal area the player receiving the ball shoots quickly on goal.

5. Check that your defense spreads out to mark and challenge each player.

Corner Kick and Shoot (Figure 12.10)

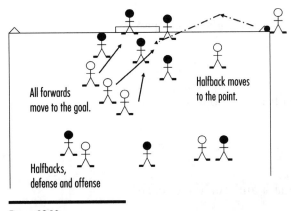

All forwards
move to the goal.

Halfback moves
to the point.

Halfbacks,
defense and offense

Figure 12.10
Corner Kick and Shoot

Purpose: This drill teaches your team how to properly execute a corner kick and how to defend against one. The principle of this drill is the same no matter how many players you use.

Preparation: Use a goal, or use cones to mark the perimeter of the goal. Place a cone at each corner of the field in line with the goal you are using to mark the corner flags.

Player needs: Players taking corner kicks need balls.

Drill execution: Choose a player to take the corner kick, and give that player a ball. Line up your other offensive players so they are at the rear, or far post of the goal. By having them at the rear of the goal, they are facing the kicker and as the kicker moves they can also move toward the goal as a team. This makes it difficult for the defense to cover every player. If players are just standing, they can easily be covered. Run the drill using both corners and multiple players kicking the ball.

Coaching Tips

1. Tell the player kicking the ball to make sure the kick is in the goal box area but out from the goalkeeper. Too close to the goal gives the goalkeeper the advantage. If the goalkeeper has to move out of the goal area, it increases the chance of scoring.

2. Watch the goalkeeper to make sure he or she either moves to the ball if it is possible to get it or stays in the goal if it is not possible to reach the ball.

3. Check that all offensive players move as a team with each player going to an open space in front of the goal.

4. Make sure the defense moves to cover the offense and to also get the ball out of the goal area as fast as possible. When the ball comes out, it should be to the side of the field, not in the center of the field.

5. Watch your halfbacks to ensure they are in position to return the ball to the goal area if they are on offense or move the ball down the field if they are on defense.

Throw-In and Shoot   (Figure 12.11)

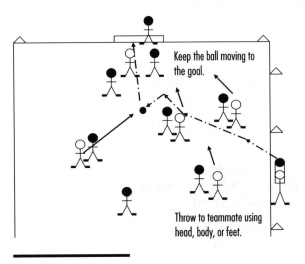

Keep the ball moving to the goal.

Throw to teammate using head, body, or feet.

Figure 12.11
Throw-In and Shoot

Purpose: This drill teaches the throw-in. There are normally more throw-ins during a game than any other dead ball situation. Being able to gain an advantage with this skill is a must to win.

Preparation: Use a goal, or set up cones to mark the perimeter of the goal. Place cones on the goal line and to mark the corner flags. Place cones in a line to mark the touchline.

Player needs: Players making the throw-in need a ball.

Drill execution: Place a player on the touchline to throw in the ball. If your players do not have the strength to throw the ball far, have them throw the ball down the line, toward your goal. The ball should stay between the touchline and not be more than four feet off the line. If your team can throw the ball with distance, you are not limited to where the ball can be thrown.

Coaching Tips

1. Make sure the player doing the throw-in keeps his or her feet on the ground and that the ball comes over the head with equal pressure so it travels straight away from the thrower.

2. If the throw is down the line, make sure your players are in positions so the player throwing the ball can see their whole bodies. They should not be behind another player.

3. If the throw-in is going out into the field, make sure all of the players are moving to open space so they have room to receive the ball and move or pass the ball.

4. See that the ball moves quickly after it is received.

5. Watch that the player throwing in the ball moves quickly onto the field to get into position to assist with the play.

6. Watch your defensive players. They should move to capture the ball or keep the ball out of the center of the field. They shouldn't let the offensive players turn the ball.

Goal Kick   (Figure 12.12)

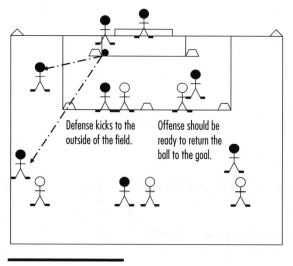

Defense kicks to the
outside of the field.

Offense should be
ready to return the
ball to the goal.

Figure 12.12
Goal Kick

Purpose: Goal kicks are similar to throw-ins in terms of the number performed during a game. Your team has to be able to clear the ball during a goal kick. Your team also must be able to capture the ball if the opposing team is kicking.

Preparation: Use a goal, or use cones to mark the perimeter of the goal. Use cones to mark the corner flags on the goal end of the field. In addition, use saucer cones to mark the corners of the goal box and the line of the penalty box.

Player needs: The player performing the goal kick needs a ball.

Drill execution: Place the ball in the goal box. Switch sides so your players are prepared no matter which side of the goal box is used for the kick. Normally you would not use the goalkeeper to take the kick. This keeps the goalkeeper in the goal in case of a quick return of the ball. If your players are young and don't have the strength to place the ball down the field, the kick should be to the outside of the penalty box. If the player can place the ball down the field, he or she should still kick to the outside, but the best is to kick to an open player. Use different defensive players to kick the ball to see who has the best kicks.

Coaching Tips

1. Make sure your team does not get into a hurry during a goal kick. It is better to make a good kick than trying to gain an advantage and perform a quick kick that results in a bad kick where the ball can be easily returned.

2. Have the player doing the kick look over the field to see who is open. Your field players should be moving to open spaces.

3. Watch that your defensive players move to receive the ball from the player doing the goal kick.

4. With younger players, place your forwards on the penalty box line since the kick is often short. Remember, they cannot enter the penalty box until the ball has crossed the penalty box line.

5. See that the goalkeeper remains in the goal box area and is prepared to field the ball if it is returned after the goal kick.

Pass and Shoot (Figure 12.13)

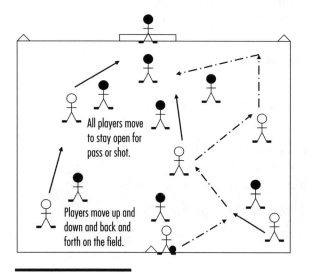

All players move to stay open for pass or shot.

Players move up and down and back and forth on the field.

Figure 12.13
Pass and Shoot

Purpose: This drill allows your players to make on-field passing decisions that will move the ball down the field and create a shooting opportunity.

Preparation: Use a goal, or set up cones to mark the perimeter of the goal. Use cones to mark the corner flags. Place a cone at midfield to mark the starting point of the drill.

Player needs: You need one ball for this drill.

Drill execution: Your offense can start the drill with a kickoff or with a pass downfield. Encourage your offense to move all over the field. They generally get in the habit of dribbling straight to the goal. Make them move right and left so they move all over the field. This gets the defense moving and creates openings for the offense. Your defense must communicate so that all offensive players are covered. As the ball moves down the field, either have your players center the ball or, if open, shoot on goal.

Coaching Tips

1. Teach the player with the ball to move to open space. Do not let that player go directly at a defensive player.

2. If the player with the ball is approached by a defensive player, make sure he or she passes while the other player is two to three steps away. Holding on to the ball too long will result in losing the ball. Passing too early will allow the defense to capture the ball.

3. See that all offensive players are constantly moving so they are always open and so the player with the ball can see their whole bodies. Offensive players cannot stay behind defensive players and get to the ball first.

4. Have the defense move with the ball and stay in a proper formation that keeps the offensive players from getting open.

5. When the defense gets the ball, make sure they pass the ball out of the defense and not just kick it down the field not knowing who it is going to.

Chip and Shoot   (Figure 12.14)

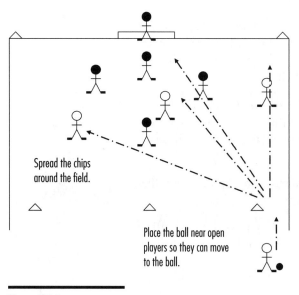

Spread the chips around the field.

Place the ball near open players so they can move to the ball.

Figure 12.14
Chip and Shoot

Purpose: This drill apples to all playing situations and can be performed during play or on a dead ball situation. Your players must be able to use the chip to advance the ball and create shooting opportunities.

Preparation: Use a goal, or use cones to mark the perimeter of the goal. Use cones to mark the corner flags on the goal end of the field. Place a cone on the right, left, and center of the field to mark the point of the chip.

Player needs: One ball is needed for the player doing the chip.

Drill execution: Set up your defense and offense to simulate an actual game situation. Have the player with the ball dribble to the cone. After reaching the cone, that player chips the ball to an open player somewhere down or across the field. Switch players doing the chip so you can see how all perform.

Coaching Tips

1. Make sure the player doing the chip is able to properly lift the ball. A chip must go into the air and over the defensive players.

2. Be sure the other offensive players are moving so they are in open spaces and not behind the defensive players.

3. Check that the defense stays balanced across the field since they do not know where the ball is going to go.

4. Make sure the chips are scattered around the field so all players know they can receive the ball and will stay open.

5. Be sure that when open the player with the ball shoots on goal. The shot must be taken quickly before the defense can react to cover it.

Goal Kick and Return   (Figure 12.15)

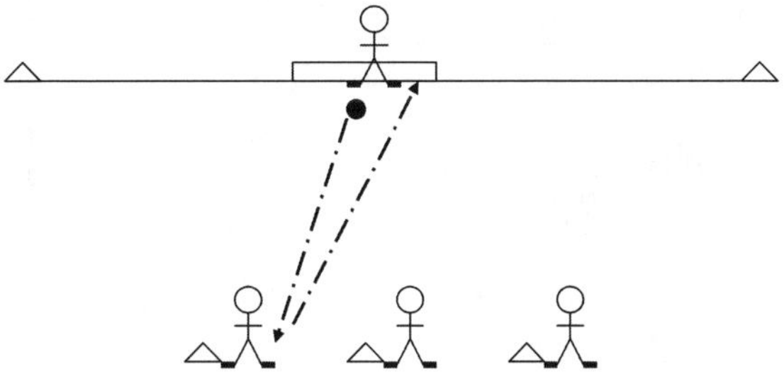

Purpose: This drill teaches players how to receive a hard-kicked ball and quickly shoot on goal.

Preparation: Use a goal, or use cones to mark the perimeter of the goal. Use cones to mark the corner flags on the goal end of the field.

Player needs: Each player needs a ball.

Figure 12.15
Goal Kick and Return

Drill execution: Set up three cones just back from the penalty box line. Have three lines with a player on each cone. The goalkeeper will kick the ball on the ground as hard as possible to the player on the cone. That player centers and shoots. The goalkeeper will capture the ball and kick it to the next player in line. The players will move to another line after each shot on goal.

Coaching Tips

1. Make sure your goalkeeper kicks the ball hard to the player waiting for the ball.

2. Watch that the player receiving the ball moves to center on the ball, gets it under control quickly, and then shoots on goal. Do not allow more than two touches on the ball before the shot.

3. See that shots are hard and away from the goalkeeper.

Corner Kick Accuracy and Shoot (Figure 12.16)

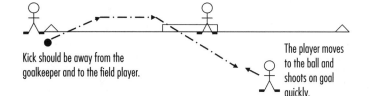

Kick should be away from the
goalkeeper and to the field player.

The player moves
to the ball and
shoots on goal
quickly.

Figure 12.16
Corner Kick Accuracy
and Shoot

Purpose: This drill improves the accuracy of the corner kick and also helps your players move to adjust on the ball coming from the kick.

Preparation: Use a goal, or use cones to mark the perimeter of the goal. Use cones to mark the corner flags. Split your team into two groups. One will be making the kick, and one will be taking the shot on goal.

Player needs: The player making the kick needs a ball.

Drill execution: Place one player on the corner to perform the corner kick. The player receiving the ball and shooting on goal will be at the back of the goal ready to move to the ball. The kick should be placed where the goalkeeper cannot reach the ball but the player waiting for the ball can easily do so. Rotate the players so they go from kicking to receiving. Rotate to the opposite corner after everyone has performed at one corner.

Coaching Tips

1. Watch that the kick is accurate. That means the ball is placed in the proper position and at the correct distance.

2. Watch that the player receiving the ball moves to center on the ball and is in a position to shoot.

3. Make sure the player receiving the ball quickly controls the ball and shoots. This player can use head, body, or feet.

4. Have the goalkeeper move to the ball if he or she can reach it. The goalkeeper can grab the ball or punch the ball out of the goal area.

Chip or Shoot (Figure 12.17)

Purpose: This is a shooting on goal drill. It gives each player the opportunity to learn when to chip to the goal and when to shoot directly on goal.

Preparation: Use a goal, or set up cones to mark the perimeter of the goal. Use cones to limit how close the players can get to the goal before shooting. Move the cones so the players take shots close to and far from the goal.

Player needs: Each player needs a ball.

Drill execution: Have each player dribble to the cone and shoot as soon as he or she reaches the cone. If the cones are close to the goal, the shot can be on the ground or in the air so the ball goes to the upper right or left of the goal. If the cones are farther from the goal, the player can chip to the goal. Line up players around the face of the goal and move down the line quickly.

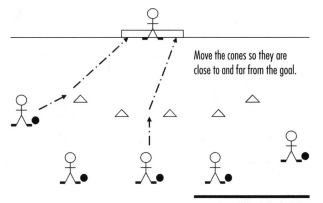

Move the cones so they are close to and far from the goal.

Figure 12.17
Chip or Shoot

Coaching Tips

1. Make sure that as the players approach the cones, they have control of the ball.

2. Tell players that when reaching the cones, they must shoot on goal. The ball should be shot away from the goalkeeper.

3. Watch for proper shooting techniques. If the players are close, they should shoot to the lower or upper sides of the goal. If the players are shooting from a distance, they should shoot for the upper portions of the goal.

Dribble, Clear, and Shoot   (Figure 12.18)

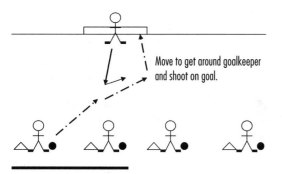

Move to get around goalkeeper and shoot on goal.

Figure 12.18
Dribble, Clear, and Shoot

Purpose: This drill is a one-on-one with the goalkeeper. The player must get past the goalkeeper before shooting on goal. This is a great drill to improve offensive moves.

Preparation: Use a goal, or use cones to mark the perimeter of the goal. Place cones around the face of the goal approximately at the penalty box line.

Player needs: Each player needs a ball.

Drill execution: Starting on the left or the right, have the first player dribble toward the goal. As the goalkeeper comes out to challenge the player, the player must move around the goalkeeper to get a shot on goal. When open the player takes the shot.

Coaching Tips

1. Watch the players as they dribble toward the goal to ensure they maintain control of the ball. They cannot kick the ball and run to it. They must keep the ball near them and in control.

2. Observe players' moves when they get near the goalkeeper. They should move right or left to make the goalkeeper chase them. Once the goalkeeper is on the move, then they can create the opening to be able to shoot.

Marking a Player   (Figure 12.19)

Purpose: This drill teaches players how to be better on defense. They play man-to-man, or one-on-one, while on defense, staying with their players. When their team gets the ball, they break away and become offense. When their team loses the ball, they must quickly pick up the players they are marking.

Preparation: Use two goals, or use cones to mark the perimeters of the goals. Use additional cones to mark the perimeter of the playing area. Break the teams into two separate teams. Team each of the players with an opposing player. Try to match the skills of your players.

Player needs: Players should have different shirts to distinguish the two teams.

Drill execution: Start play by throwing the ball into the air. The players closest to the ball will go to it and try to capture the ball. The player that captures the ball is now the offense. The opposing team is the defense. Each player shadows the player he or she is marking and tries to get the ball. The team with the ball tries to move to the goal and score. When the opposing team gets the ball, the players on the team that lost the ball quickly move to mark their players. Every player should be covered. When a goal is scored, restart play by throwing the ball. Do not use a goalkeeper for this drill.

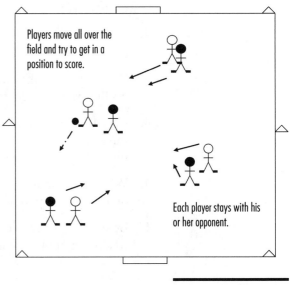

Players move all over the field and try to get in a position to score.

Each player stays with his or her opponent.

Figure 12.19
Marking a Player

Coaching Tips

1. When the ball is thrown to start play, make sure the players nearest the ball go to it. The whole team should not move to the ball, just the players nearest it.

2. After one player captures and gains control of the ball, make sure that player moves to open space with the ball or passes to a teammate.

3. Watch the defensive players to make sure they are staying with the players they were designated to mark.

4. Check to see that the player trying to capture the ball gives immediate pursuit and forces the player to the outside of the field or forces the player to give up the ball or takes the ball away from the other player.

5. When the opposing team captures the ball, make sure the other team quickly picks up their players and marks them closely.

6. Be sure no players are standing around. All players should be moving to shadow their players or, if on offense, to get open for a pass.

Indirect Kick (Figures 12.20 and 12.21)

Purpose: This drill teaches your team how to properly execute an indirect penalty kick. If proper technique is used, an indirect kick is a great opportunity to score.

Preparation: Use a goal, or use cones to mark the perimeter of the goal. Divide your team into two separate teams, one offense and one defense. Place different colored shirts on the players so they know who is on offense and who is on defense. Start the drill from a dead ball situation. The illustrations show how to accomplish this drill, but you can use multiple methods to conduct this drill. Tell your players to look for openings around, over, or through the wall. Go with the best option.

Player needs: Players wear different colored shirts to distinguish teams.

Drill execution: Place your defense so they build a wall, blocking the goal. The defensive players not in the goal must mark the remaining offensive players and shadow them as they move. The offense starts the play and shoots on goal. After the play has finished with either a goal or the ball going to the opposing team, stop play and set up the field for another try.

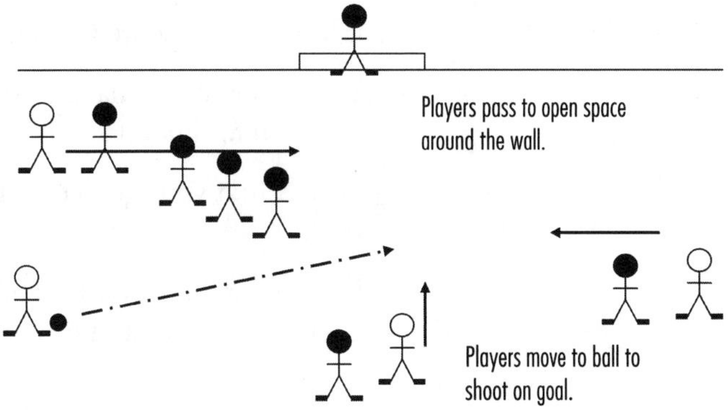

Players pass to open space around the wall.

Players move to ball to shoot on goal.

Figure 12.20
Indirect Kick,
Around the Wall

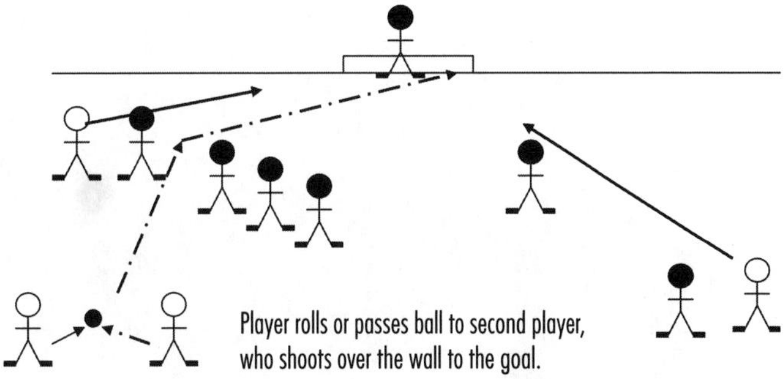

Player rolls or passes ball to second player, who shoots over the wall to the goal.

Figure 12.21
Indirect Kick,
Over the Wall

Coaching Tips

1. Make sure your goalkeeper directs the movement of the wall so the players in the wall move to block a direct opening to the goal.

2. Check your defense to make sure all offensive players are covered.

3. When play starts, make sure your offense moves to receive the ball or to get open to shoot on goal.

4. Watch that your goalkeeper moves to cut the angle of the shot to the goal.

5. Make sure the ball is touched by a second player before going into the goal since this is an indirect kick.

Direct Kick   (Figure 12.22)

Purpose: Use this drill to teach your team how to properly execute a direct penalty kick. A direct kick is a great opportunity to score.

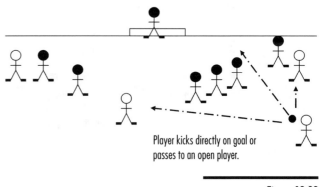

Player kicks directly on goal or passes to an open player.

Figure 12.22
Direct Kick

Preparation: Use a goal, or use cones to mark the perimeter of the goal. Divide your team into offense and defense. Place different colored shirts on the players so they know who is on offense and who is on defense. Start the drill from a dead ball situation. You can use multiple methods to conduct this drill. The two methods used in the indirect kick can be used as well as a direct shot on goal. (See Figures 12.20 and 12.21.)

Player needs: Players wear different colored shirts to distinguish teams.

Drill execution: Place your defense so they build a wall, blocking the goal. The defensive players not in the goal must mark the remaining offensive players and shadow them as they move. The offense starts the play and shoots on goal. After the play has finished with either a goal or the ball going to the opposing team, stop play and set up the field for another try.

Coaching Tips

1. Make sure your goalkeeper directs the movement of the wall so the players in the wall move to block a direct opening to the goal.

2. Check your defense to make sure all offensive players are covered.

3. When play starts, make sure your offense moves to receive the ball or get open to shoot on goal.

4. Watch that your goalkeeper moves to cut the angle of the shot to the goal.

5. Make sure your team uses different techniques so the defense does not know what is going to happen.

Zone Play   (Figure 12.23)

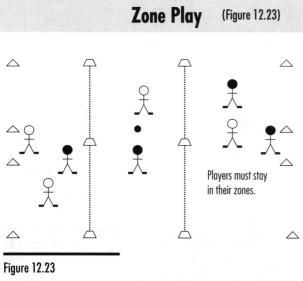

Players must stay
in their zones.

Figure 12.23
Zone Play

Purpose: This drill teaches players to stay in their areas of the field and to pass to other players.

Preparation: Use two goals, or use cones to mark the perimeters of the goals. Divide the playing area into three equal sections using saucer cones. Place an equal number of offensive and defensive players on the field, but you can switch the number of offensive or defensive players in each section or zone. You can use as few as two or as many as six players in each zone. The more players you use, the bigger layout you will need.

Player needs: Only one ball is required. Players wear different colored shirts to distinguish teams.

Drill execution: Place your players in each zone. Start play by throwing the ball into the center zone. The players in each zone cannot move into another zone. They can move freely in their own zone but can only pass to another zone. Both teams play offense and defense. The object is for players to get the ball to their teammates so they can shoot on goal. Place a goalkeeper in each goal, or play without goalkeepers. If using a goalkeeper, that person can only throw the ball into the zone he or she is in.

Coaching Tips

1. Watch that your players do not move out of their zones with the ball. They can only pass into another zone.

2. Make sure the players in the other zones move to get open since the ball can be passed forward or backward into any zone.

3. Watch for proper offensive and defensive moves on and off the ball.

4. Make sure the passes are accurate and with proper speed.

5. If a player has an opening to shoot, make sure the shot is quick and accurate.

CHAPTER 13

Goalkeeper Drills

Training the goalkeeper takes more than just letting that player play in the goal during practice while you are running other drills. Goalkeepers need to know how to catch the ball, how to punch the ball, when to move after the ball, and where to position themselves in the goal.

Bringing your goalkeeper to practice approximately 30 minutes prior to the arrival of the other players gives you a chance to work one-on-one. You can also do this by splitting the goalkeeper away from the rest of the team and letting your assistant coach work with the goalkeeper or run drills with the rest of the team. Either way you need to work directly with your goalkeeper to develop skills. Many of the drills mentioned in other chapters used the goalkeeper, which gives them additional training. But first a goalkeeper needs to know what he or she is required to do and how to do it.

Drills

Ground Catch (Figures 13.1 and 13.2)

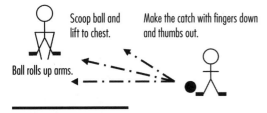

Scoop ball and lift to chest.

Make the catch with fingers down and thumbs out.

Ball rolls up arms.

Figure 13.1
Ground Catch

When the ball is coming in below the waist, the fingers are pointing down and the thumbs are to the outside.

When the ball is coming in above the waist, the fingers are pointing up and the thumbs are to the inside.

Figure 13.2
Hand Positions for
Catching Ball

Purpose: This drill teaches the goalkeeper how to catch and scoop the ball when it is coming on the ground.

Preparation: You need a ball and the goalkeeper.

Player needs: The goalkeeper can use goalkeeper gloves.

Drill execution: Place the ball on the ground, and kick it at the goalkeeper. The goalkeeper bends down, lets the ball roll into his or her hands, and then scoops it up to the chest to hold the ball. Kick the ball to the left, right, and center so the goalkeeper learns to move to the ball.

Coaching Tips

1. Make sure the goalkeeper moves into the direct path of the ball and is centered on the ball.

2. Watch to see that the goalkeeper places his or her hands so the fingers are pointing down and the thumbs are pointing out as the ball approaches. The ball should roll into the hands.

3. After the goalkeeper has the ball in his or her hands, be sure the goalkeeper pulls the ball to the chest to maintain control of the ball.

In the Air Catch   (Figure 13.3)

Purpose: This drill teaches the goalkeeper how to catch and control the ball when it is coming in the air.

Preparation: You need a ball and the goalkeeper.

Player needs: The goalkeeper can use goalkeeper gloves.

Drill execution: Place the ball on the ground, and kick it in the air to the goalkeeper, or, for a more accurate placement of the ball, toss it. The goalkeeper should move to center on the ball and place his or her hands so the ball is caught. The hands will be behind the ball with the fingers pointing up and the thumbs pointing inward toward each other. Throw the ball high to the left, right, and center so the goalkeeper learns to move to the ball.

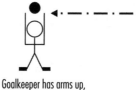

Goalkeeper has arms up, fingers pointing up, and thumbs pointing inward.

Throw the ball to the goalkeeper so it is above the waist.

Figure 13.3

In the Air Catch

Coaching Tips

1. Make sure the goalkeeper moves into the direct path of the ball and is centered on the ball.

2. When the ball reaches the goalkeeper, be sure the goalkeeper places his or her hands so the fingers are pointing up and the thumbs are pointing in. The hands should be to the rear of the ball so the ball does not travel through the hands.

3. After the goalkeeper has the ball in his or her hands, make sure the player pulls the ball into or down to the chest to maintain control of the ball.

Movement to the Ball (Figures 13.4, 13.5, and 13.6)

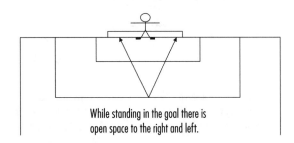

While standing in the goal there is open space to the right and left.

Figure 13.4
Standing in the Goal

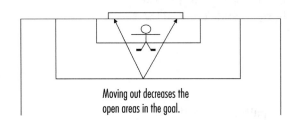

Moving out decreases the open areas in the goal.

Figure 13.5
Moving Farther Out from the Goal

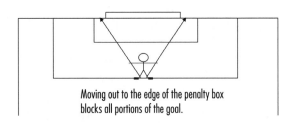

Moving out to the edge of the penalty box blocks all portions of the goal.

Figure 13.6
Blocking the Entire Goal

Purpose: The drills used in Figures 13.4–13.6 show how the goalkeeper should move to cut down the angle of the ball in relation to the goal. Using this drill allows the goalkeeper to gain the advantage by blocking access to the goal opening.

Preparation: Use a goal, or use cones to mark the perimeter of the goal.

Player needs: None

Drill execution: Place yourself in the goal, and have your goalkeeper move outside the goal area to approximately the penalty box area. Place your arms straight out to the side, and move into the three positions illustrated in Figures 13.4, 13.5, and 13.6. Your goalkeeper will be able to see how your arm movements block access to the goal by cutting down the open space to the goal. Repeat this movement by going away from each side of the goal since the angle will decrease faster than when moving from the center of the goal.

Coaching Tips

1. Stand inside the goal, on the goal line, and at the center of the goal. Stick out your arms and let the goalkeeper see how much room is uncovered to the sides of you.

2. Move out three steps with your arms out and let the goalkeeper see how much of the goal is now covered.

3. Move out three more steps, and the goalkeeper will see that the entire goal is covered from right to left.

4. Let your goalkeeper know that moving out of the goal is to his or her advantage.

Kick and Return   (Figure 13.7)

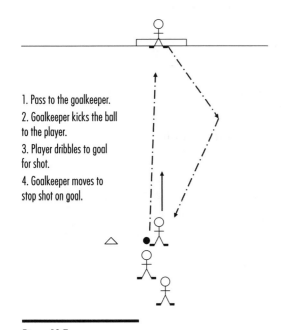

1. Pass to the goalkeeper.
2. Goalkeeper kicks the ball to the player.
3. Player dribbles to goal for shot.
4. Goalkeeper moves to stop shot on goal.

Figure 13.7
Kick and Return

Purpose: With this drill, the goalkeeper learns to move throughout the penalty area to gain possession of the ball. The drill also works on the goalkeeper's kick or throw.

Preparation: Use a goal, or use cones to mark the perimeter of the goal. Use a cone to mark the starting point for the field players, and use saucer cones to mark the perimeter of the penalty box.

Player needs: Each player needs a ball.

Drill execution: Place the goalkeeper in the goal. Line up your players at the approximate distance of your goalkeeper's kicking distance. Start the drill by having the player in the field pass or kick the ball to the goalkeeper. The goalkeeper scoops up the ball and then kicks it back or throws it back to the player who passed the ball. The player in the field has to capture the ball before the second bounce. After the player has control of the ball, that player dribbles to the goal area and tries to get a shot on goal by beating the goalkeeper.

Coaching Tips

1. Make sure the passes from the field players are hard enough to reach the goalkeeper and are accurate.

2. Be sure the goalkeeper kicks or throws the ball to the player in the field so that player does not have to chase the ball. Accuracy of the kick or throw is important.

3. Encourage the player dribbling the ball to use multiple moves to get around the goalkeeper so he or she can shoot on goal.

4. Make sure your goalkeeper stays between the player and the goal. The goalkeeper can either take possession of the ball or force the shot wide of the goal.

Corner Kick (Figure 13.8)

Purpose: This drill teaches the goal-keeper how to move for the ball during a corner kick. The goal-keeper can catch the ball or punch the ball to clear it from the goal area.

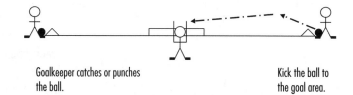

Goalkeeper catches or punches the ball.

Kick the ball to the goal area.

Figure 13.8

Corner Kick

Preparation: Use a goal, or use cones to mark the perimeter of the goal. Place cones to represent the corner flags. Have field players kick the ball.

Player needs: Each player kicking the ball needs two balls.

Drill execution: Start on one side, and have the player kick the ball from the corner to the goal area. The kick should be in front of the goal, approximately five steps out from the goal opening. When the ball is kicked, have the goalkeeper move to the ball. The goalkeeper tries to catch the ball. If the ball is high or outside the opening of the goal too much, have the goal-keeper punch the ball to clear it. Rotate sides on each kick.

Coaching Tips

1. Make sure the players kicking the ball place it in the correct spot. If they are not sure where to kick the ball, stand where the kick should be with both hands in the air. Tell them to kick to your hands. As they kick, move out of the goalkeeper's way.

2. Watch the goalkeeper to make sure he or she moves to the ball and there is no hesitation.

3. See that the goalkeeper properly judges the distance of the kick. This will improve with practice.

4. Make sure the goalkeeper uses the proper technique. It is best to catch the ball. If the ball is high or the goalkeeper has to move a distance and cannot catch the ball, have him or her punch the ball so it clears the goal area.

Penalty Kick   (Figure 13.9)

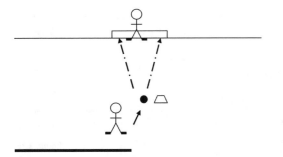

Figure 13.9
Penalty Kick

Purpose: This drill teaches the goalkeeper how to respond to a penalty kick.

Preparation: Use a goal, or use cones to mark the perimeter of the goal. Use a saucer cone to mark the penalty spot. Select two or three players to take the penalty kick.

Player needs: Each player taking a kick needs to have a ball.

Drill execution: Have the player taking the kick place the ball next to the penalty mark. Have the goalkeeper get on the goal line and prepare for the kick. When the ball is kicked, the goalkeeper moves to catch or block the shot. Repeat with each new kicker.

Coaching Tips

1. Make sure players taking the kick keep their eyes on the ball and move to the ball after the kick. If the ball bounces back, they can play the ball again.

2. Watch the goalkeeper to ensure he or she is on the goal line and ready for the kick.

3. Check that the goalkeeper reacts as soon as the ball is kicked.

4. Make sure the goalkeeper does not move prior to the kick.

5. Be sure the player kicking the ball places it to the far left or right of the goal to keep the ball at the extreme reach of the goalkeeper.

Throw and Return   (Figure 13.10)

Purpose: This drill teaches the goalkeeper to throw the ball with accuracy. It also allows the goalkeeper to play a shot on goal.

Preparation: Use a goal, or use cones to mark the perimeter of the goal. Place cones near the penalty box area. Line up your players so they are outside the penalty area and spaced across the field.

Player needs: Each player needs a ball.

Drill execution: Start with one player. That player passes the ball to the goalkeeper. The goalkeeper catches the ball and then throws the ball back to the player who originally passed the ball. The player gains control of the thrown ball and then dribbles up to the cones and shoots on

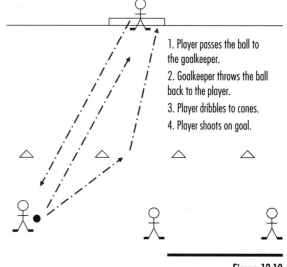

1. Player passes the ball to the goalkeeper.
2. Goalkeeper throws the ball back to the player.
3. Player dribbles to cones.
4. Player shoots on goal.

Figure 13.10
Throw and Return

goal. The goalkeeper plays the shot on goal. Move down the line so the goalkeeper is required to throw to all points on the field and is required to field the ball from different locations.

Coaching Tips

1. Check to see that the passes from the field players are hard enough to reach the goalkeeper and are accurate.

2. Make sure the goalkeeper throws the ball to the player in the field so that player does not have to chase the ball. Throwing accuracy and distance are important.

3. See that the player dribbling the ball moves to the cones and then shoots the ball away from the goalkeeper.

4. Make sure your goalkeeper moves with the player to protect the goal.

CHAPTER 14

Conditioning Drills

Many coaches overlook the importance of conditioning drills. They don't feel they have enough time during their practice, and, as a result, conditioning drills are not done. Most drills in this book require running and, therefore, do some conditioning. But just adding a few minutes of conditioning to each practice will pay big dividends in the long run.

As your players reach the end of the game, they become tired. They are unable to move as well, and their brains do not react as fast. The team that is in the best condition can often overcome better teams who are out of condition. Many games are won in the last few minutes of play due to proper conditioning. The first time you are faced with just enough players to field a team, you will realize just how important proper conditioning is.

Many conditioning drills are running off the ball type of drills. If you can incorporate drills that use passing and dribbling, you can accomplish more than one objective during the short time frame you have available.

Drills

Pass and Run   (Figure 14.1)

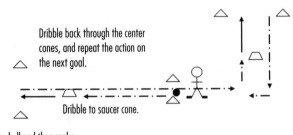

Dribble back through the center cones, and repeat the action on the next goal.

Dribble to saucer cone.

Pass the ball and then make a hard run to goal to receive the ball.

Figure 14.1
Pass and Run

Purpose: This is a simple conditioning drill that requires players to move with the ball. They dribble, pass, and run.

Preparation: Use two goals, or use cones to mark the perimeters of the two goals. Place these goals away from each other, one at each end of the field. In the middle of the field and between the two goals, place two cones so they are in the center of the field. Fifteen steps out of each goal, and centered on the goal, place a saucer cone.

Player needs: All players must have a ball.

Drill execution: Start each player one at a time from the two center cones. Start each player so he or she is approximately 10 steps behind the player in front. All players must start dribbling from the center cones. They dribble at a slow jog to the saucer cone in front of a goal. When they reach the cone, they pass the ball to the goal. As soon as they pass the ball, they must run to overtake the ball and be in the goal before the ball reaches the goal. When they get the ball, they dribble back through the center cones and go to the second goal. They must be aware of other players and move around them.

Coaching Tips

1. Watch your players to make sure they do not walk when dribbling.

2. See that your players stay clear of each other and are aware of the other players on the field.

3. Check that the pass is hard enough to get to the goal but not so hard that players cannot catch and overtake it. Players must learn touch and receive their own passes.

4. Run six shots on each goal, and watch to see which players are tiring the fastest. They are the ones who need the most conditioning.

Move with or Without Ball   (Figure 14.2)

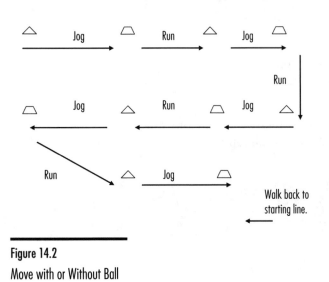

Figure 14.2
Move with or Without Ball

Purpose: This is a good cardiovascular drill to build stamina. It requires a mixture of short jogs and runs and can be done with or without the ball. If done with the ball, it is good to teach your players the ability to move fast and then slow while maintaining control of the ball.

Preparation: Place 10 cones around the field. Alternate the tower cones and the saucer cones. Place the cones so there are four on one line, four on the second line, and two on the third line. There should be 10 steps between cones.

Player needs: Each player needs a ball if you are doing this drill using the ball.

Drill execution: Start on the front line. The first cone is a tower cone. That is a jog cone. When the player reaches the saucer cone, they run hard to the next tower cone and then jog. They repeat this throughout the drill. Start with two repetitions of this drill, and as players' conditioning improves add one repetition at a time. After reaching the last cone, players walk back to the starting point.

Coaching Tips

1. If using the ball, make sure your players don't kick the ball and run to it. They must maintain control.

2. Watch that when reaching the saucer cone the player goes into a hard run and does not continue to jog.

Run Then Jog   (Figure 14.3)

Purpose: In this conditioning drill, players move around cones rather than in a straight line. It can be done with or without the ball.

Preparation: Set 10 cones around the field at staggered locations. Vary the distance between cones.

Player needs: Each player needs a ball if you are doing this drill using one.

Drill execution: Players jog through the cones first. The next time through, they run. Keep your players moving so there are only two or three steps between each player.

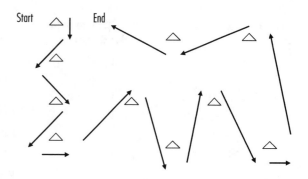

Figure 14.3
Run Then Jog

Coaching Tips

1. If using a ball to dribble, make sure the players maintain control of the ball.

2. Keep the players separated, but have multiple players running the course at the same time.

3. During the jog portion of the course, watch that the players do not walk.

Beat the Ball (Figure 14.4)

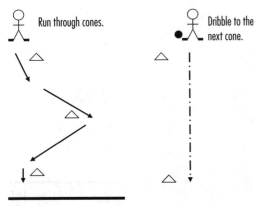

Figure 14.4
Beat the Ball

Purpose: This drill is used for conditioning and for speed dribbling.

Preparation: Place three cones in a bent line. The distance between the cones should be 10 to 15 steps each. In the second line, place two cones, one at the start and one at the finish.

Player needs: Each player on the line with two cones needs a ball.

Drill execution: Split your team into two squads. One group will be behind the multiple cones and one group behind the two cones. The group behind the two cones has the ball and is doing the dribbling. The players behind the multiple cones are running. Blow the whistle to start the drill. Each player takes off. The player dribbling goes straight down the field. The player running has to go around the cones. This is a race to see which player can outrun another player. Run this drill as teams against each other. Keep track of who wins each event, and then switch players to the other set of cones.

Coaching Tips

1. Watch that the player with the ball does not kick the ball and run to it.

2. Check to see if the player off the ball, the one running, is constantly beating the player with the ball. If that happens, either add cones or stagger the cones more until it is an equal match.

Move to the Front (Figure 14.5)

Purpose: This is a formation run that requires players to sprint to the front of the line.

Preparation: Use cones to mark the running perimeter.

Player needs: None

Drill execution: Place the team in formation, two abreast. They will do a slow jog. Blow the whistle, and the two rear players sprint to the front of the formation. When they reach the front, they step into line and become the front two. Blow the whistle again for the next two to sprint from the rear to the front. Keep this up for the whole run. Make at least two circuits around the field.

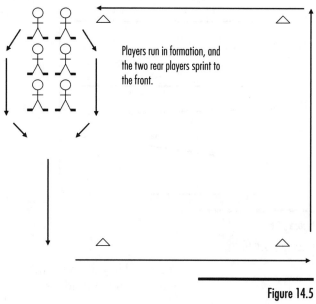

Players run in formation, and the two rear players sprint to the front.

Figure 14.5

Move to the Front

Coaching Tips

1. Make sure the jog is at a smooth pace and that the players stay in formation.

2. When the two rear players move to the front, make sure they run hard to get there fast.

Cross Field Jog/Run (Figure 14.6)

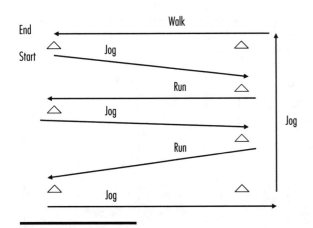

Figure 14.6
Cross Field Jog/Run

Purpose: This conditioning drill alternates the jog and the run. Dribbling can be included if you want your players to have more time on the ball.

Preparation: Set up seven cones in the course of the run/jog. Place three cones on the start side and four cones on the opposite side.

Player needs: If you are making this a dribbling and conditioning drill, each player needs a ball.

Drill execution: Start your players at one end of the field. They start with a jog across the field and then a full run back to the next cone. They do this until they reach the corner cone. At that point they jog to the end and side of the field and walk the last end of the field.

Coaching Tips

1. If your players are using a ball, make sure they maintain control of the ball during the jog and the fast run.

2. Watch that your players do not walk during the jog or the run portions.

Station Run   (Figure 14.7)

Purpose: Use this drill to build cardiovascular endurance. It is not used with a ball.

Preparation: Set up eight cones. Place four in a straight line from left to right. Go out from the first cone 10 steps and place a cone. Place a cone out from the second cone 20 steps, the third cone 30 steps, and the fourth cone 40 steps.

Player needs: None

Drill execution: Start with station one. Run hard to the cone and walk back. Repeat at each station. The distance gets farther and requires more endurance. After a player has completed the run, let him or her rest until it is that player's time again. Start with doing the drill one time, and work up until your players can go three or four times without wearing out.

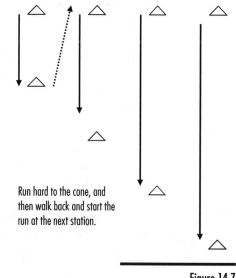

Run hard to the cone, and then walk back and start the run at the next station.

Figure 14.7
Station Run

Coaching Tips

1. Make sure the run is hard to the cones at each station.

2. See that your players walk back to start the next station and do not jog.

Jump Cones   (Figure 14.8)

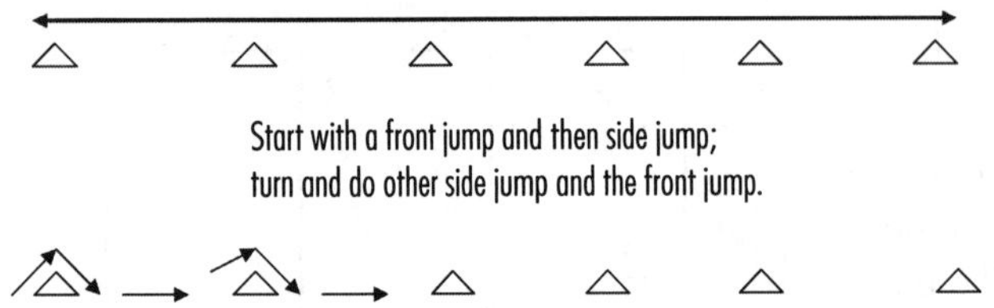

Start with a front jump and then side jump;
turn and do other side jump and the front jump.

Figure 14.8
Jump Cones

Purpose: A conditioning drill, this drill also develops the lateral jump.

Preparation: Set up multiple lines of six cones each, and break your team into equal players on each set of cones.

Player needs: None

Drill execution: Each player will do four sets of jumps over the cones. They will do this as fast as they can while maintaining their balance. Start with jumping over the cones on a full run while facing forward. Return down the cones jumping sideways; then reverse and come back jumping sideways facing the opposite direction. Finish with another full run facing the cones. The cones should be spaced 10 steps apart to allow for running and jumping.

Coaching Tips

1. Encourage your players to get height on their jumps.

2. Watch that your players run hard between the cones and take them in stride rather than stopping to make the jump.

Front/Back Race   (Figure 14.9)

Purpose: This drill provides conditioning and helps players learn to move backward with balance.

Preparation: Set up two sets of six cones each. Split the team into two groups.

Player needs: None

Drill execution: Pit the two teams against each other. The players must run forward to a cone and then backward to the next cone. They continue switching back and forth through all of the cones. When players reach the end cone, they return. When a player reaches the original starting point, the next player in line takes off and runs the course switching front to back.

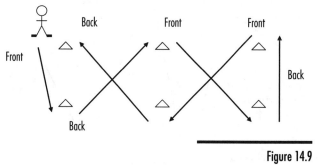

Figure 14.9
Front/Back Race

Coaching Tips

1. Encourage your players to move as fast as they can and still maintain balance.

2. Do not let players stop. When players fall, get them back up and back into the race.

Touch Cone (Figure 14.10)

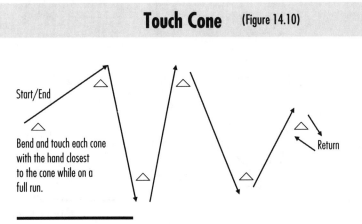

Start/End

Bend and touch each cone
with the hand closest
to the cone while on a
full run.

Return

Figure 14.10
Touch Cone

Purpose: This is a running drill that requires the player to bend down and touch the cone while on a full run.

Preparation: Set up multiple courses using a cone as a starting point and five more cones to lay out each course. Stagger the cones so the player has to run to the right and the left.

Player needs: None

Drill execution: Start the first player running toward the first cone. As that player goes around the cone, he or she bends down and touches the cone with the hand closest to it. Players continue this through the end of the cones. Then they turn back and repeat the course until they return to the starting point.

Coaching Tips

1. Make sure players go around each cone and do not just go to the front of the cone.

2. Encourage your players to touch the cones but not knock them over. As their speed increases more cones will be knocked over. Place someone to the sides of the cones to set them back up when players knock them over.

3. Do not let your players stop running to touch the cones.

CHAPTER 15

Position Play, Formations, and Fun Drills

Playing formations is a necessity in soccer as well as many other sports. The better the play is executed while maintaining a balanced formation, the better your team will perform. Practically any formation can be used if that formation provides balance and support throughout the entire field.

Diamond/Triangle Position

The most basic field setup is the diamond/triangle position. No matter what formation you use, it must incorporate balance and support. Using the diamond/triangle position ensures your team meets all requirements. The diamond/triangle position is simple and means that the player with the ball always has someone to pass to no matter where that player is on the field. These outlets will be in the form of a diamond or a triangle.

Figure 15.1 shows the diamond and the triangle for just a few players, but you can easily see that all players are in either a

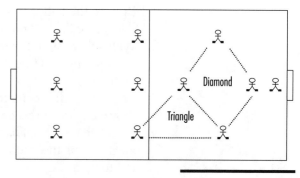

Figure 15.1
Diamond/Triangle Position

diamond or triangle position, which provides balance and support for all players. Make sure your players hold their balanced positions so they will always be in a situation where they can support the player with the ball.

Position Play

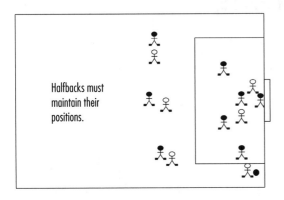

Halfbacks must maintain their positions.

Forwards and fullbacks must maintain balance and support.

Figure 15.2

Position Play

Although it may go by many different names, the term *position play* means a controlled scrimmage. The players move the ball down the field, usually in a half field setup, but rather than just let the players play you constantly stop play to point out mistakes. (See Figure 15.2.) It may be players are out of position, or dribbling too much and not passing, or a multitude of other mistakes that must be corrected.

By letting your offense play against your defense you can work all areas at the same time. Listed below are the things you need to look for. If you see a mistake, blow the whistle and stop play to point out the mistake. Correct the mistake, and then start over again. If the same players are always being corrected, your comments and the pressure from other players will quickly fix the problem.

1. Be sure the ball is moved to the outside of the field by the offense as they move the ball down the field.
2. Watch that your other offensive players stay onside and move to get into open positions. The player with the ball must be able to see their whole bodies.
3. See if the ball is centered properly and that the other offensive players move to gain possession of the ball and shoot to score.
4. Check that your halfbacks are in position and do not move into the goal area, leaving the midfield open. They should return the ball if it comes out to them.
5. Watch the defense to ensure they move to force the players to the outside yet maintain balance and coverage across the field.
6. Be sure the defensive halfbacks stay ready to receive the ball or keep the offensive halfbacks from returning the ball into the goal area.
7. Watch that the goalkeeper moves to protect the goal.

Formations

Any player grouping that provides support and balance is considered a good formation. The following formations are commonly used, but use a formation that best utilizes the strengths of your team. Formations are counted or labeled from the defense to the offense. A 4-3-3 formation means four fullbacks, three halfbacks, and three forwards. The goalkeeper is not in the equation since all formations use a goalkeeper.

All great formations put more players in the center of the field than on the outside or wings. This provides center strength and also forces the play to the outside of the field. For the offense, moving the ball down the sides of the field means less opposition.

4-3-3 Formation

This formation, shown in Figure 15.3, is the most commonly used formation because it provides strength throughout the entire field. It allows for a strong defense, midfield, and offense.

4-4-2 Formation

The 4-4-2 formation, shown in Figure 15.4, is commonly used when the opposing team has a strong offense or when your team has gotten a good lead and you want to maintain the lead by providing more defense than offense. You will have a strong midfield and defense.

Fun Drills

It is always good to be able to reward your players, especially if they have been working hard and really improving their play. The best drills allow them to have fun and at the same time improve their skills, but any drill that allows them to have fun can be used.

Volleyball/Tennis Soccer

If you practice near a park or have access to an area that has a volleyball or tennis net, let your players play either game using a soccer ball. The rules are basically the same as in volleyball or tennis except the players can only use their feet, knees, head, or other parts of their body. They cannot use their hands. Place your goalkeeper on one team and your backup goalkeeper on the other team. They can use their hands but cannot catch the ball. Also, there is no limit on the number of touches to the ball. Only the team serving can

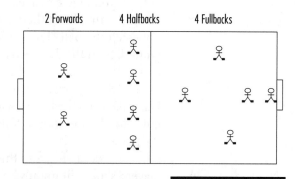

Figure 15.3
4-3-3 Formation

Figure 15.4
4-4-2 Formation

score. If one team serves the soccer ball and the other team misses, that is a point. If the team serves and then misses the ball when it is returned, the serve goes to the other team.

Try to balance your players so each side has equal skills. This makes the game more interesting and more fun. You will find that the team will love to play this game, and you will also find out that they develop improved touch on the ball.

Juggling

Juggling the ball is another fun game. This can be done individually or as a team. If you are doing it with individuals, have each player count his or her touches on the ball. Each player tries to out-juggle the other players. Many players will want to just juggle on their knees. Make them use knees, feet, and head. Be prepared for some players to go for a long time while others will only get a few touches on the ball before they lose control. All players will improve with experience.

If you juggle as a team, place everyone in a circle and put two goalkeepers in the middle of the circle. The goalkeepers can use their hands but cannot catch the ball. The soccer ball has to keep moving and cannot touch the ground. Start the drill by having one of the goalkeepers in the center throw the ball in the air to one of the players in the circle. That player will kick or head the ball. The person nearest to the ball moves to it and again uses a kick or a header to keep the ball moving. As a coach, you stand off to the side and count out loud the number of touches. When the ball touches the ground, restart the game.

Besides being fun, this drill teaches touch and control on the ball. The players' skills will improve while they have fun.

Heading

Spread the players out around the field. Let each player use his or her own ball to continuously head the ball. A player can only use the head to keep the ball in motion. Each player will count his or her own touches on the ball by yelling out the number. See who can do the most touches just using their heads. This drill is fun and teaches players to control the touch on the ball using their heads.

Throw-In

Make a competition out of throw-ins. Break the team into two groups. Set up a cone or series of cones side by side as a target. Mark a place on the field for the players to stand on opposite sides of the cones, facing each other. Set the distance based upon how far your players can throw. Let the first group throw at the cones. The team scores one point for every time the ball hits one of the cones. After each player on the first team has done a throw-in, the second team picks up the balls and takes their turns throwing. Do at least 10 repetitions for each side. The team with the most hits, or points, wins the game.

This may seem to be a very simple drill, but it is a great drill to have fun and also develop accuracy on the throw-in.

Glossary

Advantage clause: A soccer rule that gives the referee the right to have a team or player continue play after a foul was committed by the opposing team. The foul is not called if calling the foul would take the advantage away from the player or team in possession of the ball.

Age: This is used to determine which age group a child will participate in. A date, usually the end of July or August 1st, is set to ensure all children in each group are near the same age.

Alignment: How the players are positioned on the field, normally associated with a playing formation. Alignment must provide balance throughout the field.

Arc: This term is most frequently used to describe the penalty box arc, which is the arc at the top of the penalty box. It can also refer to the quarter circle, which is sometimes called the corner arc.

Arc of concentration: An area extending from each goalpost through the corner of each goal box and each penalty area box and going out to the separate touchlines. This is the area from which most goals are scored. The defense must try to keep the ball out of this area.

Assist: A pass that precedes the scoring of a goal. When a player makes a pass to the player who scored.

Assistant referees (Linesmen): Two people who assist the on-field referee by controlling the touchline and looking for offside infractions. Each assistant referee has a flag that is raised when an infraction occurs.

Attack: A team has the ball and is on the offense, attempting to score. An attack can be done by a single player or a team. It doesn't matter where the ball is on the field. If the team is moving the ball to score, it is an attack.

Attacker: A player on the team that has possession of the ball.

Back: Defensive player that plays nearest the goal. Backs are often referred to as fullbacks or left, right, or center backs.

Back pass: Passing the ball backward instead of forward.

Back post: The goalpost located the farthest from a particular player. This is also referred to as the far post.

Back side: The side of the goal opposite from where the ball is being played.

Balance: How a team addresses the other team's players. In means how they play in relation to the player with the ball.

Ball: A soccer ball comes in three sizes: number 3, 4, or 5. The size used depends on the age of the player.

Banana kick: Kicking the ball into the air and making it curve like a banana. The curve is created because of sidespin on the ball. This kick is also referred to as bending the ball.

Beat: Getting past a player.

Bicycle kick: A specialty kick often referred to as a scissor kick. Used by advanced players, it is accomplished by falling backward and bringing both feet off the ground. The kick is made by bringing the feet forward, over the head, and striking the ball with a foot while the player is upside-down in the air.

Blind side: The area behind a player.

Boot: This word has two meanings in soccer. It refers to kicking the ball and is also another name for a soccer shoe.

Bounce: When the ball hits the ground and rebounds back into the air.

Boundary lines: Marked lines on a soccer field that indicate the outer perimeter of the playing area. The boundary lines are a maximum of five inches wide.

Box: Term used most commonly for the penalty box area of the field. Sometimes used to indicate the goal box area.

Breakaway: When a player gets past the defense and moves on the goal undefended, creating a one-on-one situation with the goalkeeper.

Bylaws: The rules and regulations used by soccer leagues to establish local policy.

Caps: An old term derived from swapping hats at the end of an international game. It now refers to the number of official international games a player has played in for his or her national team.

Card: A card pulled from the referee's pocket and shown by that referee to indicate a serious infraction of the rules. Two colors are used. A red card removes a player from the field and the game, and a yellow card is a warning that further infractions will result in expulsion from the game.

Carry: Another word for *dribble.*

Caution: The action of showing a yellow card by the referee.

Center: To kick the ball from the side of the field to the center. This is normally a tactic used while near the opponent's goal. Centering gets the ball into the arc of concentration, which increases the chance of scoring.

Center circle: The area in the center of the field used for starting play. The ball is placed in this area at the beginning of the game and at the beginning of the second half. The center circle is also used to start play after a team scores. The opposing team cannot enter the center circle until the kickoff team has played the ball. The maximum size of the center circle is 10 yards from the center to the outside of the circle.

Center pass: Passing the ball from the outside to the center of the field.

Center spot: A mark to indicate the middle of the center circle. This is where the ball is placed for kickoffs to start or restart play.

Challenge: A term used to indicate when a defender tries to steal the ball from an offensive player.

Charge: An act of rushing a player and hitting that player by using the body. This is a foul.

Chest trap: When the ball is received on the chest and falls to the player's feet so that player can play the ball.

Chip: When the ball is kicked into the air as a pass or shot. Executed properly, the kick is just hard enough to go over the head of the opponent.

Clear: To get the ball and remove it from an area as quickly as possible.

Coach: The person in charge of training the players and directing them during their games.

Cone: A plastic device with a larger bottom than top that is used during practice to mark specific areas. Often a bright color like international orange.

Contain: A method used to limit or restrict the opponent's ability to move or advance.

Corner arc: A quarter circle marking that is on each corner of the field. The ball is placed in this area to restart play after the ball is kicked over the end line by the defending team.

Corner flag: A flag mounted on a pole placed at the exact corner of the field. This flag, which should be a minimum of five feet tall, enables the players to see the maximum boundary of the field from a distance.

Corner kick: The method used to restart play after the ball has gone out of bounds by crossing the end line and was last touched by the defensive team

(team guarding the goal). The offensive team puts the ball into play by kicking it out of the corner quarter arc.

Counterattack: A term indicating that a team has gained possession of the ball by a turnover and has stopped the attack by the opposing team. This is the start of that team's attack, which "counters" the other team's attack.

Cover: A defensive term that refers to staying close to an opponent.

Creating space: To move away from opponents in order to open up some space to make it easier to pass or dribble the ball.

Cross: To send the ball from the outside of the field to directly in front of the goal. It can also mean to move the ball from one side of the field to the opposite side.

Cross bar: The top post of the goal.

Danger zone: The area directly in front of the goal, often referred to as the arc of concentration. This is the area from which most goals are scored.

Dangerous play: Any type of play or an action taken by a player that can result in an injury to another player.

Defender: A player primarily responsible for defending the goal.

Defense: The actions required to protect the goal and prevent the opposing team from scoring.

Deflection: When the ball hits and bounces off of another player or the goalposts.

Deliver the ball: Making a good pass to a teammate.

Depart: When a player leaves the field of play. Players are not allowed to enter or depart the field without official referee permission.

Depth: The placement of players on the field. Good depth is when players are evenly dispersed from end to end of the field.

Depth of field: The length of the field from one end line to the other end line.

Direct kick: The type of kick used after a major foul has been committed. The ball can be kicked directly into the goal. When the ball enters the goal by crossing over the goal line, a goal is scored. This is indicated by the referee pointing an arm directly toward the goal.

Distribute: Used to indicate a goalkeeper's kick. The goalkeeper gives the ball to a specific player or players on the field.

Draw: A game that ends with a tie score.

Dribble: Moving the soccer ball with the feet. Proper dribbling allows the player to maintain control of the ball.

Drills: The activities used during a practice to teach players how to further develop their soccer skills.

Drop ball: The technique used by the referee to restart the game. The referee drops the ball between two opposing players; neither player can kick the ball until it has touched the ground.

Dropkick: A type of kick used by the goalkeeper. The goalkeeper drops the ball to the ground and kicks it after it bounces back up.

Encroachment: A term used to indicate a defender too close to the offensive player on a start or restart. A predetermined distance must be given to allow the ball to be put back into play.

End line: The boundary line at each end of the field. This is also referred to as the goal line where it crosses inside the limits of the goal.

Enter: A player can only enter the field during a restart and only with the permission of the referee.

Equipment: The items used by the coach or player to practice or play soccer.

Far post: The goalpost farthest from a player. This post is commonly referred to as the back post.

Fast break: Advancing the ball past the defense and toward the goal before the defense can respond.

Feint: Making a fake move to beat a defensive player.

Field: The marked area on which teams play soccer. Fields vary in size depending upon availability of land. Small-sized games are played on reduced-size fields.

Field player: The players on the game field.

Field the ball: A term used to play the ball or to put the ball into play.

FIFA: Fédération Internationale de Futbol Association, the international governing agency for soccer.

Finish: The act of ending a play by scoring.

Flank: The outside of the field (wing), closest to the touchline.

Flick: A term used to mean that the ball is being relayed or moved on to another player without being stopped. This can be done by a head or foot pass.

Foot trap: A technique to stop the ball using the foot.

Formation: A term referring to the placement of the players on the field. Formations are always indicated by the count, starting with the fullbacks. The goalkeeper is not included in the count, and the count can never exceed a maximum of 10. A 4-4-2 formation indicates 4 fullbacks, 4 midfielders, and 2 forwards for a total of 10 players.

Forward: Name of a player located closest to the opponent's goal and who has the primary duty of scoring.

Forward pass: Passing the ball so it moves down the field toward the opponent's goal.

Foul: Any infraction of the rules.

Free kick: Any kick awarded to a team as the result of an infraction of the rules.

Futbol/Football: The official name of the game of soccer. It is commonly used in every country except the United States and Canada, where it is called soccer.

Game clock: The official elapsed time that remains in the game is the game time. The official time is kept by the referee. The referee holds the game clock. Even if there is a spectator clock it is not the official time.

Game time: The amount of time for a designated game. Full games are split into two 45-minute halves. Time is reduced for small-sided games.

Give and go: With this move, a player passes the ball and then moves to a position to again accept the ball; sometimes called a wall pass.

Goal: The goal is the rectangular area at each end of the field that has a maximum width of eight yards, a maximum depth of six yards, and a maximum height of eight feet. The front edge of the goal is directly on the end line. The back of the goal is covered by a net to catch the ball after it has entered the goal.

Goal box: The small marked rectangular area located directly in front of the goal. The goal box is a maximum of 20 yards wide and 6 yards deep.

Goalkeeper (Goalie, Keeper): The player who works directly in front of the goal. When the goalkeeper stops the ball, the stop is called a save. The goalkeeper can only use his or her hands while inside the penalty area. No other player on the team can use the hands while on the field of play. The goalkeeper is required to wear a different color jersey to distinguish himself or herself from the other players on the field.

Goal kick: One method used to restart play after the ball has gone out of play over the end line and was last touched by the offensive team. The defensive team places the ball in the goal box and kicks the ball out of the penalty box to restart play.

Goal line: The portion of the end line located between the goalposts.

Goalposts: The vertical poles on the goal.

Goal scored: When the ball travels completely over the goal line, this is a score. Each goal scored counts as one point.

Goal side: A term used to indicate the placement of a defensive player between the offensive player and the goal.

Half: The soccer game is split into two equal halves of time. These halves are divided by a period called halftime.

Halfback: A player positioned in the formation between the fullbacks and the forwards. Also referred to as a midfielder.

Half line: The line marked on the field that divides it into two equal halves. The center circle is on this line.

Halftime: The period of time between the first half and second half of the game during which players receive instructions, rest, and drink liquids.

Half volley: A type of kick performed by allowing the ball to bounce on the ground and then kicking it while it is in the air.

Hand ball: An infraction of the rules caused by a player touching the ball with his or her hands or arms while on the field of play.

Hat trick: Three goals scored in one game by a single player.

Header: A skill where a player uses the head to pass the ball or shoot on goal.

Holding: The act of grabbing another player by the body or clothing to stop that player from moving freely.

Home team: The team that normally plays on the field where the game is being played. In the case of league play where all teams play on the same field, a team is designated as the home team. The home team normally furnishes the ball and linesmen, if needed.

In bound: Throwing the ball into the field of play.

In bounds: When the ball remains inside the boundaries of the field.

Indirect kick: A type of kick used to restart play after a minor foul has been committed. The ball must take an indirect route to the goal. To do this, the ball must be touched by another player after the original kick and before going into the goal.

Injury: When a player is hurt while on the field of play; play continues until the referee stops it.

Injury time: When a player is hurt while on the field of play the referee will stop the game and the game clock. The amount of injury time that elapses while the game is stopped can be added to the end of that half of play of the game. This is at the discretion of the referee.

In play: When the ball is being played while inside the boundaries of the field.

Instep: The part of the foot that normally kicks the soccer ball. This can be on the inside of the foot or on the laces of the shoe.

Jersey: The shirts worn on the field by a soccer player. Each team wears shirts that are different colors. The goalkeeper is required to wear a shirt that is distinctively different than those worn by the other players on the field.

Juggling: The act of bouncing and controlling the ball using the feet, thighs, and head. The ball is moved from one part of the body to the other while maintaining control of it.

Keeper: A slang name for the goalkeeper.

Kick: Striking and moving the ball using the foot.

Kickball: A term used to indicate players running all over the field and kicking the ball rather than playing soccer.

Kickoff: The method used to start a game or restart play after a goal is scored.

Knock off the ball: A technique used by a defensive player to move the opponent away from the ball. This is done by having the defensive player keep his or her arm straight along the side and using pressure to move the offensive player off the ball. Elbows and arms that are sticking out or shoving the player violate the rules.

Laces: Refers to the top of the foot, which is where the laces of the shoe are located.

Laws: The rules of the game that govern the play and conduct of the soccer players.

Leading pass: A kicked or passed ball that ends up in front of another teammate. This type of pass allows that player to move to the ball without changing speed or direction.

Linesmen: The two people that assist the referee by controlling the touchline and looking for offside infractions. These people are assistant referees.

Long ball: A kick by an offensive player that ends up with the ball traveling beyond the group of defensive players on the field. This allows a teammate to move to the ball unopposed.

Major foul: Any infraction of the rules that is dangerous to players on the field.

Manager: The player that assists the team coach by making telephone calls, arranging rides for players, and other tasks, allowing the coach to concentrate on training players.

Mark: A term used for a player placed in a position where he or she plays one-on-one with an opposing player.

Match: The name for the actual soccer game.

Midfielder: A player located on the field in a position between the fullbacks and the forwards. Also referred to as a halfback.

Minor foul: An infraction of the rules, but an infraction that is not considered a dangerous play by the referee.

Near post: The goalpost closest to the player with the ball.

Net: The type of mesh covering used on the back and sides of the goal. This is a net that can be seen through but stops the ball when it enters the goal.

Nutmeg: A name for the action when a player kicks the ball between the legs of an opposing player.

Obstruction: When an on-field player uses the body to play or interfere with another player rather than playing the ball. This is an infraction of the rules.

Offense: When a player or players on the same team move the ball toward the opposing goal trying to score.

Officials: The referee and linesmen or assistant referees. These are the only officials that have responsibility for controlling and governing the game.

Offsides: A rule intended to keep an offensive player from standing in front of the goal of the opposing team. An offensive player must have one defender between him or her and the goalkeeper when the ball is kicked by a teammate.

One touch: A pass or shot by a player who only touches the ball one time. This is done by shooting or passing without dribbling.

Open space: When a player moves to an area on the field where there is no other player.

Opponent: The opposite team your team is playing.

Out of play: A term used to indicate when the soccer ball or a player is outside the boundaries of the playing field.

Overlap: The act of running past another teammate in order to advance down the field and get in position for a pass or shot.

Own goal: The name for the goal your team is defending.

Pace: The speed of the movement of the ball or player. It is also used to indicate the speed of the game.

Pass: Moving the soccer ball from one player to another using foot, head, or other legal part of the body.

Penalty arc: A portion of a circle located on the outside center of the penalty area. This area is not part of the penalty area, but it is an area that players must stay outside of to maintain a specified distance from the ball.

Penalty area: The rectangular area directly in front of the goal that serves as the boundary where the goalkeeper is able to touch the soccer ball using his or her hands.

Penalty kick: The kick used to restart play when a major foul has been committed inside the penalty area by the team defending the goal. To restart, the ball is placed on the penalty mark. One player from the team fouled enters the penalty area to take the kick. Only the goalkeeper from the defending team and the player kicking the ball are allowed inside the penalty area.

Penalty mark: A mark placed on the field inside of the penalty area. This mark is where the ball is placed for a kick after a direct foul has been committed inside the penalty area.

Pitch: A term used to denote the soccer playing field. This term is used for most soccer fields throughout the world.

Player: A member of a team engaged in the game of soccer.

Play on: The term used by the referee to inform players to continue play. This is normally heard as a result of the implementation of the advantage rule.

Point: The unit used to denote a goal scored. There is one point counted per each goal scored.

Position play: This is a controlled scrimmage used to teach players how to stay, and hold, their positions on the field during game play.

Possession: A term that indicates your team has control of the ball.

Power shot: A hard shot normally taken on goal in an attempt to score.

Practice: The activity used to teach and condition soccer players.

Pressure: Keeping close contact with a player to keep that player from advancing or scoring.

Quarter circle: The quarter circle mark used on each corner of the field. The ball is placed in this area to restart play after the ball has been kicked over the end line by the defending team.

Rainbow kick: A specialty kick done by putting the ball between the feet, using one foot to roll the ball up the back of the leg, and using the heel of the other foot to kick the ball over the player's head from behind. The ball travels from the rear of the player to the front, taking an arc similar to a rainbow.

Rebound: When the ball hits the goalposts or another player and bounces back into the field of play.

Receiving: The action of gathering or collecting the ball.

Recover: When a team loses the ball and the players are caught out of position. The players must get back into the proper position.

Red card: A red card, about the size of a playing card, used by the referee to inform a player and team that the player is being ejected from the game. This player cannot be replaced by the team, and the team must play one player short.

Redirect: Changing the direction of a moving ball by using a pass or a kick.

Referee: The official on the field responsible for enforcing the laws of the game.

Restart: A term used to indicate when the ball is put back into play after a stoppage of the game.

Rules and regulations: The laws and amended laws used by the soccer leagues to establish local policy.

Run: The move made by a player, with or without the ball, to get into another position.

Save: A term used to indicate that the goalkeeper stopped the ball from going into the goal.

Score: The points earned by each team. Each goal counts as one point.

Scrimmage: When a team plays another team in a practice game.

Settle: The act of controlling the ball.

Shield: Protecting the ball from an opposing player. This is done by the first player placing his or her body between the opposing player and the ball.

Shin guards: A protective device worn under the socks to protect players when they are kicked in the shins.

Shirt: The jersey worn by the soccer player.

Shoes: The footwear worn by soccer players. Soccer shoes are designed to give the player traction and allow the player to kick and dribble without the toe of the shoe snagging on the ground. There is no cleat underneath the toe of the shoe. The cleats are dispersed throughout the sole of the shoe.

Shoot-out: An action used when the game ends with a tied score. Each team gets five kicks, using different players that are one-on-one with the goalkeeper. Each team sends one player at a time to shoot on goal. The kicks are alternated between teams. After each team has taken five shots, the team that has scored the most is declared the winner. If the teams remain tied after the initial five players, the alternating kicks will continue until one team is able to score and the other does not.

Short: A term meaning to play with fewer players than normal.

Shorts: The short pants worn by soccer players. The color of the shorts can either match or contrast with the jerseys worn by the players.

Shot: When the soccer ball is kicked, headed, or passed toward the goal by an offensive player.

Shoulder charge: A legal play that allows a defender to press against the player with the ball to move that player off the ball.

Skills: The psychomotor actions a player is required to learn to properly perform the techniques in the game of soccer.

Slide tackle: A move where one player slides or moves into the ball to take or knock the ball away from an opponent.

Small sided: A term used to indicate play when there are fewer than the standard 11 players.

Socks: Garments that cover the feet and the shin guards on the players. Socks must be knee-high and can match or contrast in color with the uniform.

Square: Positioning of a player so that he or she is directly to the right or left of the player with the ball.

Start: Denotes the beginning of the game at the first half and the second half.

Steal: To remove or take the soccer ball away from an opponent.

Stoppage time: The time added to a game for any stoppages. This additional time can be the result of injury, ball out of play, substitution, or other events deemed as a loss of playing time by the referee.

Stopper: The defender who plays in front of the other defenders and is positioned closest to the center line.

Strategy: The approach used by the coach to formulate the game plan.

Striker: The center forward on the offense.

Strong side: The side of the field the ball is on.

Substitution: The act of replacing one player on the field with another player who has been off the field. This can only be done during certain restarts in the game and with referee approval.

Support: When a player or players move into a position to assist and support a teammate with the ball.

Sweeper: The sole defender who is the last defender and plays in front of the goalkeeper.

Tackle: The action used by a player when he or she slides into the ball to take or knock it away from an opponent.

Tactics: The skills and techniques used during game play. Also refers to set plays used in a game.

Techniques: Skills that enable a player to understand and participate in the game.

Through pass: The act of passing the soccer ball so it goes beyond the defense into open space or to another teammate. This is a pass used to give an offensive player the ball as that player moves behind a defensive player.

Throw-in: The method used to restart the game after the ball has traveled out of bounds over the touchline. The ball is thrown in by the team that did not cause the ball to go off the field.

Time out: *Time out* is not an official term used in soccer, but it is often used to indicate when the game clock kept by the referee is stopped.

Toe kick: An improper kick used in soccer. This is used to denote when the ball is struck by the toe of the shoe. It is an inaccurate type of kick.

Touchline: The line that marks each side of the field. This is the boundary for the width of the field. This line is also referred to as the side line.

Trap: Stopping the ball to gain control. This action can be done using many different parts of the body.

Tripping: Causing someone to stumble or fall. This is a major infraction of the rules.

Turn over: Losing the ball while the game is in play and having that ball go to the other team.

Under: Sometimes identified as "U-". Used in the game of soccer to denote the age of the players. *Under* is used in conjunction with a number. U-8 means the players must be under the age of eight

Uniform: The shirt, shorts, and socks worn by team players.

Victory: Winning the game.

Vision: The ability of a player to see openings and other players while on the field of play.

Volley: Kicking the ball while the ball is still traveling through the air.

Wall: The positioning of players, side by side, to form a line to prevent a kick from going through to the goal.

Wall pass: A technique using two or more players to pass the ball around the opponent. Also called the give and go pass.

Width: Field layout of players from side to side on the field. Good width is even spacing covering from touchline to touchline.

Width of field: The area from one side of the field to the other side.

Wing: The outside area of the field that is closest to the touchline.

Winger: Normally a forward who plays on the right- and left-hand side of the field. The term can also be used to describe any outside player.

Winning: Scoring more points than the opposing team.

World Cup: Soccer games played every four years by professional teams from all participating and qualifying countries in the world. This is the largest sports event in the world and is controlled by the FIFA.

Yellow card: A yellow-colored card, about the size of a playing card, used by the referee to warn a player and team that the player is being cautioned for an infraction of the rules.

Zone play: When players are situated in a set area of the field that they must defend.

Index